D0280228

indian food

Das Sreedharan

photography by Peter Cassidy

quadrille

This edition first published in 2005 by **Quadrille Publishing Limited**
Alhambra House, 27-31 Charing Cross Road, London WC2H OLS

Editorial director Jane O'Shea
Creative director Helen Lewis
Managing editor Janet Illsley
Art director Vanessa Courtier
Design Ros Holder and Amanda Lerwill
Editor Jenni Muir
Photographer Peter Cassidy
Food stylist Sunil Vijayakar
Props stylist Jane Campsie
Copy editor Kathy Steer
Production Ruth Deary

Text © 2003 Das Sreedharan **Photography** © 2003 Pete Cassidy
Design and layout © 2005 Quadrille Publishing Limited

Reprinted in 2006 (twice), 2007
10 9 8 7 6 5 4

Originally published exclusively for J Sainsbury plc.

Cataloguing in Publication Data: a catalogue record for this book is available
from the British Library.

ISBN: 978 1 84400 215 3

Printed in China

Cookery notes
All spoon measures are level: 1 tsp = 5ml spoon; 1 tbsp = 15ml spoon.
Use fresh herbs and freshly ground black pepper unless otherwise suggested.
Free-range eggs are recommended and large eggs should be used except
where a different size is specified. Recipes with raw or lightly cooked eggs
should be avoided by anyone who is pregnant or in a vulnerable health group.

Contents

introduction

Although British people love to eat Indian food, many have been put off cooking it at home because they believe the dishes are too complicated and require a lot of strange ingredients. To me, this is a sad misperception. Throughout India there are many wonderful examples of simple home cooking using ingredients readily available on supermarket shelves in this country. And there is nothing I would like better than to tell you more about these recipes.

Since moving to England and establishing my first restaurant, it has been my mission to promote the kind of food I was fortunate enough to enjoy while growing up in Kerala, South India's largest state. Like most people, I still think my mother is the best cook in the world! Many of the dishes that I prepare today – whether in the restaurants, during my cookery evenings for customers, or at home with my wife Alison – are those I adored when I was young. Like many Asians, our family was vegetarian and daily meals were healthy combinations of fresh vegetables, fruits, yogurt and nuts, with many of the ingredients grown in our own garden.

Over the years I have also collected a good many recipes from friends and colleagues while travelling throughout India. The ones I have chosen for this book come from various communities with substantially different religious and cultural traditions. Like the South Indian recipes (which are themselves from a lively cultural mix), they use ingredients that are easy to find and methods that are simple and quick. There are meat dishes including Goan pork vindaloo and Kashmiri lamb rogan josh, chicken and vegetable dishes from Bengal, and many recipes using the dairy products and pulses beloved throughout North India.

In addition, I am including several of our restaurants' most popular dishes and new creations developed during my cookery evenings. I really enjoy taking ingredients such as courgette and cauliflower, which I never knew as a child, and creating new Indian dishes from them. Fusing Northern and Southern Indian cooking styles is also a great passion of mine, but that doesn't mean the resulting dishes are complicated – some of them contain as few as six ingredients.

My home state of Kerala is known as the 'spice box' of India but I have limited the range of spices in this book, so you won't have to buy more than you are comfortable with. A few Indian techniques, such as making spice blends, may seem a little daunting at first, but you will be astonished at how quick and easy they are. The blender you already use to whiz soups until smooth works equally well as a grinder for producing fragrant pastes, sauces and batters. Soon you will be doing so with confidence, as well as quickly grating fresh coconut in the food processor, and softening tamarind pulp to add a sour fruity flavour to curries.

My mother always said that no one can teach you to cook. She said: 'I will show you how I do it, but you have to learn to do it your way.' This is an important tradition in India. You should feel free to adapt the quantities of spices, oil, water and main ingredients given in these recipes to suit your own taste. I do hope that you enjoy using this book and that it inspires you to cook more often. It doesn't matter whether the food you prepare is South Indian, North Indian or Italian, I honestly believe that home cooking is the foundation of good health and happiness.

Ingredients

You won't need an extensive array of spices and authentic flavourings to prepare my recipes, but here is a guide to the special ingredients that feature in this book.

Banana leaves
Elongated banana leaves are used in South India and other tropical Asian countries to wrap foods for cooking, such as fish for steaming, in much the same way as aluminium foil is used in the West. They can also take the place of serving plates. You can buy banana leaves from specialist Asian food stores.

To use banana leaves in cooking, first soften by holding over a flame or dipping in a dish of warm water for 30 seconds. This will make the leaves pliable and easy to fold.

Chana dal
These robust yellow lentils are derived from a brown variety of pea that is skinned and split. They look very similar to yellow split lentils and have a sweet and nutty aroma. Chana dal is combined with meat in curries, ground with lamb to make a paste for kebabs, and frequently cooked with vegetables, especially squashes. In Kerala it is used to make sweet as well as savoury dishes.

Chillies
The wide range of chillies available today can be confusing, but in Keralan dishes and for the recipes featured in this book, there are only two types that you need to buy. Small dried red chillies, 2.5–3cm (1–1¼ inches) long, are available from the spice rack, and fresh green chillies, about 7.5cm (3 inches) long, are sold in the fresh produce department.

Chillies are renowned for the fiery heat they bring to dishes, and this makes some people wary of them. However, their heat can be controlled. You can bring chilli flavour to a recipe without strong heat by using the chilli whole rather than slicing or chopping it. To do this, make just one cut about two-thirds of the way along the length of the chilli to release the flavour before adding it to the pan. The seeds in the chilli are particularly hot. In recipes where chillies are sliced or chopped, I rarely deseed them but you may prefer to do so for a milder flavour.

Coconut

The large hairy brown coconut is indigenous to several areas, one of which is South India, and the freshly grated white flesh of the nut is essential to Keralan cooking. It is used in an amazing variety of ways, including vegetable side dishes, breads, curries, savoury snacks and sweet dishes, and appears in some form at every meal.

Unsweetened desiccated coconut can often be used in place of freshly grated coconut in dishes, but it has a much drier texture and the result is not as succulent. It is far better to use the fresh nut.

To extract the flesh from a fresh coconut, insert a metal skewer in the eye of the coconut and drain the water into a jug. Using a heavy tool, such as a butcher's steel or cleaver, carefully crack the shell around the middle and separate the inner nut from the hairy casing. You can then use a vegetable peeler to make long shavings of coconut flesh, or an ordinary kitchen grater to grate it. When only a small amount is required, a citrus zester will give you fine shreds quickly and easily. To prepare a substantial quantity of fresh coconut, place the pieces of coconut flesh in a food processor and process until finely chopped.

Coconut milk

Don't confuse this with the clear water inside a fresh coconut. Coconut milk is a manufactured product, made by pouring hot water over grated coconut flesh, then pushing through a sieve to give a thin white liquid. Coconut cream is similar, but has a much thicker consistency. Coconut milk is used as the base for many South Indian dishes. It is available in cans and long-life packs.

Curry leaves

Curry leaves come from a plant with the botanical name of 'Murraya koenigi' and are thought to smell and taste like curry powder. While the taste is spicy, it is also nutty, a quality brought out when the curry leaves are lightly fried in oil until just crisp. They are used as herbs in cooking, most often added whole, but sometimes chopped first. Bay leaves may look similar, but they have a very different flavour and are not an appropriate substitute. Don't hesitate to buy a substantial bunch of curry leaves when you see them on sale. For convenience, they can be stored in the freezer wrapped in foil or sealed in a polythene bag, and added to dishes as and when required.

Ghee

Highly popular in North India, ghee is the Indian version of clarified butter. That is butter which has had all its milk solids removed. The process

involves melting the butter over a low heat, then simmering it until all the moisture has evaporated and the milk solids have separated from the fat. The milk solids are then removed to leave a pure fat, which is excellent for frying at high temperatures. It also has a long shelf life – ghee is sold in cans on the supermarket shelf rather than in the fresh dairy section.

Jaggery and palm sugar
An unrefined form of sugar, jaggery is dark, sticky and crumbly. Made from the juice of crushed sugar cane, it is less sweet than ordinary white or brown sugars and has an extraordinary musky flavour. Palm sugar from countries such as Thailand has a comparable rich, complex taste and is a reasonable substitute for Indian jaggery in cooking. Brown and demerara sugars lack this earthy quality, but the recipes in this book will work if you use them.

Paneer
India's best-known cheese is often described as a 'cottage' or 'curd' cheese because it is usually freshly made in the home. However, paneer is drained and pressed, which makes it very different from the cottage and curd cheese known in Britain. Paneer's firmer texture means it can be cut into cubes, then fried or grilled until golden while still retaining its square shape. Look for it in the chiller cabinet alongside other cooking cheeses.

Plantains
Sometimes referred to as cooking bananas, plantains look rather like large bananas, but have a thicker green skin and starchier, less sweet flesh. This fruit plays an important role in South Indian cooking and several different varieties grow in Kerala alone. When green, or unripe, they are used as a vegetable in curries; when ripe they are steamed and eaten for breakfast.

Rice
Fragrant basmati rice is often regarded as the supreme variety, but we tend not to use it on a daily basis in India because it is expensive by comparison to other locally grown varieties. Basmati rice also has a unique aroma, which can be lost when combined with many strongly flavoured ingredients. The recipes in this book indicate when regular long-grain white rice is adequate.

Rice flour
Fine, white, powdery rice flour is commonly used for batters and doughs in South India, and to make soft rice noodle cakes. It can also be used as a thickening agent, in the same way as cornflour. It has a mild flavour.

Spices

Spices that feature most often in my cooking include whole brown mustard seeds, ground turmeric, cumin, coriander and cinnamon. Using mustard seeds in the way I do doesn't impart a strong mustard flavour, but a slightly crunchy texture. Turmeric is India's most widely used spice and brings a mellow flavour and golden colour to dishes. Cumin is one of the most versatile spices. It can take on different flavours depending on how it is treated – used whole, ground, toasted, fried or raw. Garam masala, which means 'hot spices' is a convenient ready-made mix of ground spices, and is aromatic rather than fiery. Almost every Indian kitchen has its favourite blend, but most contain black peppercorns, cardamom, cinnamon, cumin, cloves and mace.

Tamarind pulp

This tart fruit is used in South Indian and Gujarati cooking as a souring agent and brings a tangy contrast to mild coconut sauces. It is also used for chutneys and drinks. Sold in dried blocks with a long shelf life, tamarind pulp needs to be soaked in hot water for about 20 minutes to soften the fruit, then pushed through a sieve to remove any seeds and fibres. The resulting liquid is stirred into dishes. Although the process of making tamarind liquid is always the same, recipes can vary in the intensity of liquid required, so the ratio of tamarind to hot water varies accordingly.

Urad dal

The small black lentils used to make urad dal are found in a variety of forms in India. In the North, the whole black lentils are favoured, while in Southern India (and in all of my recipes) the lentils are invariably skinned and split. Although these are also known as black gram dal, the term is confusing because South Indian urad dal is cream in colour. It is rather like a spice, added to dishes to provide a nutty flavour and crunchy texture.

Yogurt

Thick and creamy yogurt is made every day in homes across the Indian subcontinent and is an important part of every meal, most commonly enjoyed plain as a mild contrast to spicy food. Raitas – cooling salads made with yogurt and crunchy vegetables – are very popular. Yogurt is also often churned into cooling drinks with spices, and is the base for many desserts. In savoury cooking, its main role is as a souring agent. Any thick creamy natural yogurt will work for the recipes in this book but avoid any brands that are very sharp and acidic in flavour.

indian starters, snacks and chutneys

Mushroom and coconut uthappams

Makes 8
300g (11oz) long-grain rice
75g (3oz) urad dal
½ tsp fenugreek seeds
vegetable oil, for frying
sea salt

For the topping
100g (3½oz) mushrooms, sliced
1 red onion, peeled and finely sliced
2 green chillies
2 tbsp chopped coriander or curry
   leaves
50g (2oz) freshly grated coconut

1 Place the rice in a large bowl and cover with cold water. Place the dal and fenugreek seeds in another bowl and add cold water to cover generously. Set both bowls aside and leave to soak for at least 8 hours or overnight.
2 Drain the rice and dal, keeping them separate. Put the rice into a blender and process slowly for 2–3 minutes, gradually adding 125ml (4fl oz) water to make a smooth paste. Transfer to a large bowl. Put the dal and fenugreek seeds in the rinsed-out blender and process slowly for 5 minutes, adding 4 tbsp water to make a batter. Add to the rice paste and mix well. Add a little salt and cover with a damp cloth. Leave to ferment for 12 hours or overnight.
3 When ready to cook, the batter should have increased in volume and become a mass of small bubbles. Stir a little water into the batter to give a thick pouring consistency. Heat a griddle or large, heavy-based frying pan until very hot, then lightly brush with oil. Assemble the topping ingredients and divide into 8 portions.
4 Pour a ladleful of the batter on to the griddle and spread it out slightly with the back of a spoon until about 10cm (4 inches) in diameter, about the size and thickness of an English pancake. Top with a portion of the mushrooms, onion, chilli and coriander or curry leaves, pressing them gently into the batter, then sprinkle lightly with the coconut. Cook for 2 minutes or until the bottom is golden brown.
5 Brush the edges of the uthappam with oil and carefully turn it over with a spatula. Cook on the other side for 2–3 minutes until the batter is cooked and the onion and mushrooms have browned slightly. Remove and keep warm while you cook the remaining uthappams.
6 Serve the uthappams with coconut chutney (page 46) or as a bread-like accompaniment to 'wet' curries.

Lentil and spinach vadai

Illustrated on previous pages

Serves 4
400g (14oz) chana dal, or yellow
   split peas
200g (7oz) spinach leaves, tough
   stalks removed
1 onion, peeled and finely chopped
2 green chillies, finely sliced or
   chopped
2.5cm (1 inch) piece fresh root
   ginger, peeled and finely chopped
10 curry leaves, finely chopped
vegetable oil, for deep-frying
sea salt

1 Place the chana dal in a large bowl, cover with water and set aside to soak
for 1 hour. Meanwhile, place the spinach in a large saucepan over a low heat
with just the water clinging to the leaves after washing and cook, stirring
occasionally, for 1 minute or until just wilted. Set aside to cool, then chop
finely. Tip the soaked dal into a sieve and drain thoroughly.
2 Transfer the dal to a blender and process for 2–3 minutes to a coarse paste
– don't grind it too finely as you want some of the dal to remain whole to
give the vadai a good texture. Tip into a large bowl and add the chopped
spinach, onion, chillies, ginger, curry leaves and a little salt. Mix thoroughly
to make a thick paste.
3 Divide the mixture into portions, about the size of a golf ball, then roll
each one between your palms and gently flatten into a small round patty.
The mixture will make about 20 patties.
4 Heat the oil in a deep-fryer, wok or large, heavy-based saucepan to
180–190°C or until a cube of bread browns in 30 seconds. Deep-fry the
patties in batches for 5 minutes or until deep golden. Remove with a slotted
spoon and drain on kitchen paper. Serve hot or cold.

These crunchy lentil patties are very popular
afternoon snacks in India. They can be made
with various lentils, but this version featuring
chana dal is one of my favourites. If you can't
find chana dal, substitute yellow split peas.

Onion bhajis

Illustrated on previous page

Serves 4

2 onions, peeled and finely sliced
175g (6oz) chick pea flour
1cm (½ inch) piece fresh root ginger,
   peeled and finely chopped
½ tsp chilli powder

½ tsp ground turmeric
pinch of crushed coriander seeds
50g (2oz) coriander leaves, finely
   chopped
vegetable oil, for deep-frying
sea salt

1 In a large bowl, mix together the onion slices, chick pea flour, ginger, chilli powder, turmeric, crushed coriander seeds, coriander leaves and a little salt. Gradually mix in 500ml (16fl oz) water to make a thick batter.

2 Heat the oil in a deep-fryer, wok or large, heavy-based saucepan to 180–190°C or until a cube of bread browns in 30 seconds. Using a metal spoon, take a small portion of batter and shape roughly into a ball, then carefully drop into the hot oil and deep-fry for 3–4 minutes or until the bhaji is cooked through and has a crunchy, golden exterior. Cook the bhajis in batches of two or three, adding them to the oil one at a time. Remove with a slotted spoon and drain on kitchen paper. Serve hot.

Bhajis can be made with various vegetables, including greens, so experiment with this basic recipe.

Bonda

Serves 4

400g (14oz) potatoes, peeled and
  cubed
4 tbsp vegetable oil
1 tsp mustard seeds
1 tsp urad dal
20 curry leaves
2.5cm (1 inch) piece fresh root
  ginger, peeled and grated
2 onions, peeled and finely chopped
2 green chillies, finely sliced
1 tsp ground turmeric, plus extra
  to season
4 tbsp finely chopped coriander
  leaves
125g (4oz) chick pea flour
vegetable oil, for deep-frying
sea salt

1 Cook the potatoes in a saucepan of lightly salted water for 15 minutes or until tender, then drain and mash. Set aside.

2 Heat the 4 tbsp oil in a large frying pan. Add the mustard seeds and urad dal and cook, stirring constantly, for 1–2 minutes or until the dal turns brown. Add the curry leaves, ginger and onions and cook, stirring occasionally, for 5 minutes.

3 Add the chillies and turmeric and cook for a further minute before adding the mashed potatoes and chopped coriander leaves. Stir over a low heat for 1 minute to ensure that the ingredients are thoroughly mixed, then remove the frying pan from the heat and set aside to cool.

4 Place the chick pea flour, a pinch of turmeric and a pinch of salt in a large bowl, then gradually stir in 275ml (9fl oz) water to make a smooth batter. Whisk until thoroughly blended, then set aside for 5 minutes.

5 Divide the potato mixture into small balls about the size of a golf ball. Heat the oil in a deep-fryer, wok or large, heavy-based saucepan to 180–190°C or until a cube of bread browns in 30 seconds. Cook the bonda in batches. Dip the potato balls in the batter and carefully drop them into the hot oil one by one, making sure that the pan is not overcrowded. Deep-fry for 3–4 minutes or until golden, then remove with a slotted spoon and drain on kitchen paper. Serve hot, with coconut chutney (page 46), sweet mango chutney (page 48) or with garlic and chilli pickle (page 43).

Steamed rice and vegetable dumplings

Illustrated on previous pages

Makes 12
about 225g (8oz) rice flour
1 tbsp vegetable oil, plus extra
    to oil
sea salt

For the filling
2 tbsp vegetable oil
1 tsp mustard seeds
50g (2oz) onion, peeled and finely
    chopped
1 tsp ground coriander
½ tsp chilli powder
½ tsp ground turmeric
25g (1oz) tomatoes, chopped
40g (1½oz) peas
1 tsp freshly ground black pepper,
    or to taste

1 Put the rice flour and a little salt in a large bowl and make a well in the centre. Gradually stir in 175–250ml (6–8fl oz) warm water or just enough to make a smooth dough. Add the oil and mix to a soft dough, adding a little more flour or water if necessary.

2 For the filling, heat the oil in a large frying pan, add the mustard seeds and, as they start to pop, add the onion and a little salt. Cook for 5 minutes or until the onion is soft. Add the coriander, chilli powder and turmeric and mix well. Add the tomatoes and 4 tbsp water and cook for 2 minutes. Stir in the peas and pepper, cover and simmer gently for 10–15 minutes until well cooked. Take off the heat.

3 Oil your hands, then break off a piece of dough (about the size of a golf ball) and shape into a flat patty. Place a small spoonful of the filling in the middle of the patty and lightly fold the dough around it to enclose the filling. Gently roll into a ball and set aside on a plate. Repeat to use all the dough and filling.

4 Set a steamer over a large pan of water and bring to the boil. Put the dumplings in the steamer, cover and steam for 15 minutes or until the dough is cooked through. Serve hot or cold, allowing three each.

These savoury dumplings can be eaten as a snack at any time of the day, with a chutney or pickle. Or serve with a drizzle of spiced oil, made by frying a few curry leaves, dried red chilli, mustard seeds, coriander seeds and a pinch of chilli powder in oil until sizzling.

Spicy vegetable samosas

Illustrated on previous pages

Serves 4
250g (9oz) ready-made samosa
    pastry
vegetable oil, for deep-frying
For the filling
4 tbsp vegetable oil
1 tsp mustard seeds
2 onions, peeled and diced
1 tsp ground coriander
1 tsp chilli powder
½ tsp garam masala
½ tsp ground turmeric
2 potatoes, peeled and diced
1 carrot, peeled and diced
150g (5oz) green beans, trimmed
    and diced
150g (5oz) peas
sea salt

1 First make the filling. Heat the 4 tbsp oil in a large frying pan, add the mustard seeds and fry until they start to pop, then add the onions and fry until soft. Add the ground spices and a little salt and fry, stirring, for 1 minute. Add the vegetables, cover and cook for 15 minutes. Remove from the heat and set aside to cool.
2 Cut the samosa pastry into strips, 25 x 7.5cm (10 x 3 inches). Place 1 heaped tablespoon of filling at one end of a pastry strip, positioning it centrally. Fold a corner over the mixture to form a triangle, then continue folding in alternate directions along the strip to make a triangular parcel.
3 Heat the oil in a deep-fryer, wok or large, heavy-based saucepan to 180–190°C or until a cube of bread browns in 30 seconds. Fry the samosas, one at a time, for 2–3 minutes until golden. Drain on kitchen paper.
4 Serve the samosas hot or cold, on their own or with a pickle or chutney (pages 43–9) if you prefer.

India's best-known snacks are easy to make at home, using ready-made samosa pastry. If you can't find this, use filo instead.

Spicy lamb samosas

Serves 4

250g (9oz) ready-made samosa
  pastry

vegetable oil, for deep-frying

For the filling

5 tbsp vegetable oil

3 onions, peeled and chopped

2 tomatoes, chopped

1 tsp tomato purée

2 green chillies, finely diced

2 garlic cloves, peeled and finely
  chopped

1 tsp chilli powder

1 tsp garam masala

250g (9oz) lamb mince

100g (3½oz) potatoes, peeled and cut
  into cubes

3 tbsp chopped coriander leaves

sea salt

1 First make the filling. Heat the 4 tbsp oil in a large frying pan, add the
chopped onions and fry until soft and golden. Add the tomatoes, tomato
purée, chillies, garlic, chilli powder, garam masala and a little salt; mix well.
2 Add 250ml (8fl oz) water, stir well and bring to the boil. Stir in the lamb
mince and potatoes. Simmer, covered, for 20 minutes or until the mixture is
well cooked and thick. Stir in the chopped coriander and set aside to cool.
3 Cut the samosa pastry into strips, 25 x 7.5cm (10 x 3 inches). Place
1 heaped tablespoon of filling at one end of a pastry strip, positioning it
centrally. Fold a corner over the mixture to form a triangle, then continue
folding in alternate directions along the strip to make a triangular parcel.
4 Heat the oil in a deep-fryer, wok or large, heavy-based saucepan to
180–190°C or until a cube of bread browns in 30 seconds. Fry the samosas,
one at a time, for 2–3 minutes until golden. Drain on kitchen paper.
5 Serve the samosas hot or cold, on their own or with a pickle or chutney
(pages 43–9) if you like.

Mushroom and cashew nut samosas

Serves 4

250g (9oz) ready-made samosa
  pastry
vegetable oil, for deep-frying

For the filling

2 potatoes, peeled and cut into cubes
50g (2oz) cauliflower florets,
  chopped
3 tbsp vegetable oil
2 onions, peeled and finely sliced

2 green chillies, finely diced
75g (3oz) cashew nuts, broken into
  pieces
½ tsp ground turmeric
½ tsp garam masala
200g (7oz) mushrooms, sliced
50g (2oz) spinach leaves, tough
  stalks removed
4 tbsp chopped coriander leaves
sea salt

1 First make the filling. Boil the cubed potatoes in salted water to cover for 5 minutes. Add the chopped cauliflower and cook for 2–3 minutes, then drain thoroughly.

2 Heat the 3 tbsp oil in a large frying pan and fry the onions, chillies and cashew nuts for 4 minutes. Stir in the ground spices, then add the potato and cauliflower, mushrooms and spinach. Cook, covered, for 4 minutes; the vegetables should be slightly crunchy. Stir in the chopped coriander and set aside to cool.

3 Cut the samosa pastry into strips, 25 x 7.5cm (10 x 3 inches). Place 1 heaped tablespoon of filling at one end of a pastry strip, positioning it centrally. Fold a corner over the mixture to form a triangle, then continue folding in alternate directions along the strip to make a triangular parcel.

4 Heat the oil in a deep-fryer, wok or large, heavy-based saucepan to 180–190°C or until a cube of bread browns in 30 seconds. Fry the samosas, one at a time, for 2–3 minutes until golden. Drain on kitchen paper.

5 Serve the samosas hot or cold, on their own or with a pickle or chutney (pages 43–9) if you like.

Beetroot cutlets

Makes 6

8 tbsp vegetable oil
1 tsp mustard seeds
few curry leaves
2.5cm (1 inch) piece fresh root
　ginger, peeled and finely sliced
1 onion, peeled and finely sliced
1 tsp ground turmeric
1 tsp chilli powder

1 tsp garam masala
150g (5oz) cooked beetroot, peeled
　and finely diced
100g (3½oz) potatoes, peeled and
　finely diced
50g (2oz) peas
100ml (3½fl oz) milk
400g (14oz) breadcrumbs
sea salt

1 Heat 4 tbsp oil in a large frying pan. Add the mustard seeds and, when
they start to pop, add the curry leaves, ginger and onion. Fry for 5 minutes
or until the onion is soft.
2 Stir in the turmeric, chilli powder and garam masala. Stir in the beetroot,
potatoes and peas, then add about 100ml (3½fl oz) water and a little salt.
Cook for 10 minutes or until the vegetables are very tender. Remove the pan
from the heat and set aside to cool.
3 When the vegetable mixture is cool enough to handle, divide into 6 equal
portions and form into teardrop-shaped cutlets.
4 Pour the milk into a shallow dish and spread the breadcrumbs out on a
plate. Dip each beetroot cutlet into the milk, then into the breadcrumbs and
turn to coat evenly, gently pressing the crumbs on to the cutlets to adhere.
5 Heat the remaining oil in a clean frying pan. You may need to cook the
cutlets in two batches. Add them to the hot pan and fry for 3–5 minutes
until crisp and golden, turning frequently. Drain on kitchen paper. Serve the
cutlets hot, with kiwi fruit chutney (page 47) or date chutney (page 49).

You may associate the term cutlets with lamb
chops, but it is a different story in India where
they are savoury cakes.

Garlic and chilli pickle

Serves 8
4 tbsp vegetable oil
pinch of fenugreek seeds
100g (3½oz) garlic cloves, peeled
  and sliced
1 tsp tomato purée
1 tsp crushed mustard seeds

1 tsp chilli powder
½ tsp ground turmeric
4 green chillies, roughly chopped
200ml (7fl oz) white vinegar
1 tsp brown sugar
sea salt

1 Heat the oil in a large, non-stick frying pan. Add the fenugreek seeds and cook, stirring constantly, for 1 minute or until they turn golden. Add the garlic and cook gently, stirring occasionally, for about 5 minutes until it is tender and has started to colour.

2 Add the tomato purée, mustard seeds, chilli powder, turmeric, chillies and a little salt. Fry the mixture for 2–3 minutes, then pour in the vinegar and cook over a low heat for about 25–30 minutes until the garlic is browned and all the liquid has evaporated.

3 Stir in the sugar, then remove the pan from the heat and set aside to cool before use or storage. You can keep the pickle sealed in a screw-top jar in the refrigerator for up to 2 weeks.

This delicious, spicy pickle is an excellent accompaniment to samosas, bonda and other Indian snacks.

Shrimp pickle

Serves 4

1cm (½ inch) piece fresh root ginger,
  peeled and chopped
2 garlic cloves, peeled
½ tsp ground turmeric
1 tsp sea salt
200g (7oz) peeled shrimp or prawns,
  chopped

vegetable oil for deep-frying, plus
  4 tbsp
½ tsp mustard seeds
few curry leaves
2 green chillies, slit lengthways
1 tsp chilli powder
1 tsp mustard powder
300ml (½ pint) white wine vinegar

1 Using a small spice mill or a pestle and mortar, pound the chopped ginger and garlic together to make a paste. Set aside.

2 In a small bowl, mix together the turmeric and salt with 1 tbsp water to make a paste. Add the chopped shrimp and stir to coat.

3 Heat a 5cm (2 inch) depth of oil in a large, heavy-based saucepan or wok to 180–190°C or until a cube of bread browns in 30 seconds. Deep-fry the shrimp for 3–4 minutes until light golden, then remove with a slotted spoon and set aside to drain on kitchen paper.

4 Heat 4 tbsp oil in a large frying pan. Add the mustard seeds and, when they start to pop, add the curry leaves, chillies, chilli powder, mustard powder and the ginger-garlic paste. Cook, stirring constantly, for 1 minute or until the spices give off a toasted aroma.

5 Add the shrimp and cook, stirring constantly, for a further 2–3 minutes or until all the pieces are coated with the spice mixture. Pour in the wine vinegar and simmer, stirring occasionally, for 10 minutes or until the pickle thickens. Remove the pan from the heat and set aside to cool before serving.

This recipe is a contribution from a fishing family living in Cochin, South India.

Coconut chutney

Serves 4

1 tbsp tamarind pulp
100g (3½oz) freshly grated coconut
2 green chillies, roughly chopped
2.5cm (1 inch) piece fresh root
  ginger, peeled and sliced
1 garlic clove, peeled

2 tbsp vegetable oil
1 tsp mustard seeds
1 small onion, peeled and finely
  chopped
10 curry leaves
sea salt

1 Break up the tamarind pulp and place in a small bowl. Add 3 tbsp hot water and leave to soak for 20–30 minutes.
2 Press the mixture through a sieve to extract 3 tbsp of tamarind liquid and pour this into a blender. Add the coconut, chillies, ginger, garlic and a little salt, and process to a smooth paste.
3 Heat the oil in a small frying pan. Add the mustard seeds and, when they start to pop, stir in the onion and curry leaves. Cook over a medium heat for 2–3 minutes or until the onion is golden. Lower the heat and add the coconut mixture. Mix well and serve hot or cold.

There is nothing like a freshly made, tangy, spiced chutney to accompany special snacks, curries and rice dishes. This one is made with fresh coconut and has a sharp, clean flavour.

Kiwi fruit chutney

Serves 4

200g (7oz) kiwi fruit
1 tomato, finely chopped
2 green chillies, chopped
3 shallots, peeled and chopped
1cm (½ inch) piece fresh root ginger,
    peeled and very finely chopped
pinch of freshly ground black
    pepper
sea salt

1 Peel the kiwi fruit and cut the flesh into small pieces. Place the tomato, chillies, shallots, ginger, black pepper and a little salt in a blender and pulse briefly until the tomatoes are just lightly crushed.
2 Add the kiwi fruit a little at a time, processing slowly until you have a coarse textured chutney. Transfer to a small serving dish.

Kiwi fruit, with its sweet-sour flavour, has the ideal qualities for a fresh chutney. Try this recipe with other fruits too.

Sweet mango chutney

Serves 4

200g (7oz) sweet mango
25g (1oz) shallot or onion, peeled
    and chopped
2 green chillies, chopped
2 garlic cloves, peeled
2 tbsp curry leaves
sea salt

1 Peel the mango, cut the flesh away from the stone, then dice it and set aside. Place the shallot or onion, chillies, garlic, curry leaves and a little salt in a blender and process to a smooth paste. Add the diced mango and process to a coarse paste.

2 Transfer the mango chutney to a serving bowl, cover with cling film and chill in the refrigerator before serving.

Made with sweet fruit, this versatile chutney is reminiscent of Bombay. It tastes very different from the spicy, sour mango chutneys that are typical of my home state, Kerala.

Date chutney

Serves 4
200g (7oz) fresh dates, chopped
3 garlic cloves, peeled and chopped
2 dried red chillies
4 tbsp lime juice
2 tbsp freshly grated coconut
sea salt

1 Place the dates, garlic, chillies, lime juice, coconut and a little salt in a
blender and process to a smooth paste. Transfer to a serving bowl.

Fresh dates make a good, rich chutney. This
recipe goes particularly well with samosas and
onion bhajis.

indian soups, salads and side dishes

Keralan seafood soup

Serves 4

50g (2oz) long-grain white rice
4 tbsp vegetable oil
1 tsp mustard seeds
pinch of cumin seeds
20 curry leaves, chopped
4 garlic cloves, peeled and chopped
2.5cm (1 inch) piece fresh root
    ginger, peeled and chopped
3 green chillies, finely sliced
3 onions, peeled and chopped

½ tsp ground turmeric
½ tsp chilli powder
½ tsp crushed black pepper
250g (9oz) raw prawns, peeled,
    deveined and halved if large
200ml (7fl oz) coconut milk
To serve
4 cooked king prawns in shell
    (optional)
3 tbsp freshly grated coconut

1 Cook the rice in 350ml (12fl oz) water in a small saucepan until just tender, drain and reserve 250ml (8fl oz) of the cooking water. Set aside.
2 Heat the oil in a medium saucepan. Add the mustard seeds and, when they start to pop, add the cumin seeds, curry leaves, garlic, ginger, chillies and onions. Fry for 5 minutes or until the onions are soft. Stir in the turmeric, chilli powder and black pepper, and stir-fry for 2 minutes.
3 Add the prawns, cooked rice and the reserved cooking water. Cook over a low heat for 10 minutes or until the prawns are cooked and the soup is creamy. Add the coconut milk, bring to the boil, then lower the heat and simmer for a further 5 minutes.
4 Ladle the seafood soup into warmed bowls and top each serving with a whole cooked prawn if you like. Scatter with freshly grated coconut and serve with Indian bread, such as Malabar parathas (page 237).

This exquisite soup combines three things Kerala is particularly renowned for – spices, coconuts and seafood – and it can be varied to include any fresh seafood.

Spiced lentil soup

Serves 4

125g (4oz) split red lentils

50g (2oz) chana dal, or yellow split peas

50g (2oz) mung beans

1 onion, peeled and finely sliced

1 tomato, diced

1 green pepper, cored, deseeded and diced

50g (2oz) spinach leaves, tough stalks removed

4 garlic cloves, peeled and finely chopped

2 green chillies, finely sliced

2.5cm (1 inch) piece fresh root ginger, peeled and finely chopped

1 tsp chilli powder

1 tsp garam masala

1 tsp ground turmeric

sea salt

4 tbsp coriander leaves, finely chopped, to serve

1 Combine the lentils, chana dal, mung beans, onion, tomato, green pepper, spinach, garlic, chillies, ginger, chilli powder, garam masala, turmeric and a little salt in a saucepan.

2 Stir in 1.2 litres (2 pints) water and bring to the boil. Simmer, stirring frequently, for 20 minutes or until the pulses are thoroughly cooked.

3 Ladle the soup into warmed bowls and sprinkle chopped coriander leaves over each portion. Serve hot, with Indian bread if you like.

This soup is based on a spiced mixture of lentils and beans, and you can add potatoes to make it more filling if you like.

Spicy mixed salad

Serves 4

3 tomatoes
½ cucumber
2 apples
2 pears
2 oranges
2 bananas, peeled
50g (2oz) radishes, quartered
pinch of garam masala
1¼ tsp sea salt
½ tsp chilli powder
2 tbsp lemon juice

1 Cut the tomatoes, cucumber, apples and pears into bite-sized chunks and place in a large bowl. Peel and segment the oranges, then halve each segment and add to the bowl. Cut the bananas into chunks and toss them into the salad with the quartered radishes.
2 Sprinkle the garam masala, salt and chilli powder over the salad, then add the lemon juice and toss well. Cover and chill slightly before serving.

Salads are very popular in India, but they are usually spiked with some chilli. This recipe is very flexible – vary the spices, vegetables and fruit to taste.

Coconut and radish salad

Illustrated on previous pages

Serves 4
2 tbsp vegetable oil
1 tsp mustard seeds
1 tsp urad dal
few curry leaves
100g (3½oz) shallots, peeled and halved
3 green chillies, finely chopped
3 tbsp lemon juice
3 tbsp white wine vinegar
50g (2oz) freshly grated coconut
200g (7oz) radishes, quartered
sea salt

1 Heat the oil in a large frying pan or wok. Add the mustard seeds and, when they start to pop, add the urad dal and curry leaves. Cook, stirring constantly, for 1–2 minutes until the urad dal turns brown.
2 Add the shallots and stir-fry for 5 minutes or until they are shiny and translucent. Add the chillies and a little salt and stir-fry for 1 minute. Pour in the lemon juice and vinegar, then add the grated coconut and mix well. Remove the pan from the heat.
3 Transfer the fried mixture to a large bowl. Add the quartered radishes and toss to mix, then serve.

This salad is quick to make and has a lovely clean, fresh flavour, with a nutty crunch provided by the toasted urad dal. You can use cucumber instead of radishes, if you prefer.

Paw paw salad

Serves 4

1 small, ripe paw paw
1 guava
1 tbsp vegetable oil
½ tsp urad dal
8 shallots, peeled and finely sliced
pinch of chilli powder
4 tbsp wine or cider vinegar
pinch of sea salt
5 tbsp coconut milk
juice of 1 lemon

1 Peel, halve and deseed the paw paw and guava, then cut into cubes. Set aside in a large bowl.
2 Heat the oil in a frying pan. Add the urad dal and fry, stirring constantly, for 1–2 minutes until it turns brown, then add the shallots and sauté over a low heat for 1 minute. Sprinkle in the chilli powder, then add the vinegar and salt. Increase the heat and stir-fry for 1 minute. Remove the pan from the heat and slowly mix in the coconut milk.
3 Pour the shallot mixture over the prepared fruits, add the lemon juice and toss well. Serve cold.

In India, the tropical paw paw (also known as papaya) is included in curries, stir-fries and spicy dishes, such as this refreshing salad.

Tomato and red onion raita

Illustrated on previous pages

Serves 4
1cm (½ inch) piece fresh root ginger
3 green chillies
1 red onion, peeled
1 tomato
50g (2oz) cucumber
200g (7oz) yogurt
To serve
pinch of chilli powder
chopped coriander leaves (optional)

1 Peel and very finely chop the ginger. The easiest way to do this is to
remove the skin with a swivel vegetable peeler, then cut the ginger into thin
slices. Cut these slices into matchsticks, then into tiny dice.
2 Finely slice the green chillies into rings. Chop the red onion very finely.
Cut the tomato and cucumber into tiny cubes, discarding the seeds.
3 Put the yogurt in a large bowl. Add the tomato, cucumber, red onion,
chillies and ginger and stir to mix. Serve sprinkled with a pinch of chilli
powder and chopped coriander leaves if you like.

Raita is a cooling accompaniment, ideal to counter those fiery dishes that can take you by surprise. Red onions work well because they are milder and sweeter than most onions.

Shallot thoran

Serves 4–6

5 tbsp vegetable oil
1 tsp mustard seeds
1 tsp urad dal
12–14 curry leaves

250g (9oz) shallots, peeled and
  finely chopped
3 green chillies, finely chopped
100g (3½oz) freshly grated coconut
sea salt

1 Heat the oil in a large frying pan, add the mustard seeds and fry until they start to pop, then add the urad dal and 10 curry leaves. Cook, stirring, for 1–2 minutes or until the dal turns brown.
2 Add the shallots, chillies and a little salt, and cook for 5 minutes or until the shallots are transparent.
3 Add the freshly grated coconut and a few extra curry leaves and stir-fry for 1 minute. Serve immediately.

Thorans are lightly cooked vegetable salads, which are served as part of most Keralan meals to provide a fresh-tasting, crunchy contrast to saucy dishes.

White cabbage thoran

Serves 4–6
5 tbsp vegetable oil
1½ tbsp mustard seeds
1 tsp urad dal
10 curry leaves
3 onions, peeled and finely sliced

4 dried red chillies
1 tsp ground turmeric
1 small cabbage, cored and shredded
100g (3½oz) freshly grated coconut
sea salt

1 Heat the oil in a large frying pan, add the mustard seeds and fry until they start to pop, then add the urad dal and curry leaves. Cook, stirring, for 1–2 minutes or until the dal turns brown.
2 Add the onions and dried chillies and cook over a high heat for 1 minute, then lower the heat and cook for 5 minutes or until the onions are soft. Add the turmeric and a little salt, stirring well.
3 Stir in the cabbage, cover and cook for 10–15 minutes or until tender. Stir in the grated coconut and serve.

Thorans are often described as dry dishes, but the balance they bring to a meal is healthy and textural. The basic cooking technique is reminiscent of Chinese stir-frying.

Green bean thoran

Serves 4–6

5 tbsp vegetable oil
1 tsp mustard seeds
1 tsp urad dal
10 curry leaves
1 small onion, peeled and finely
  sliced
2 green chillies, finely diced
1 tsp ground turmeric
250g (9oz) green beans, trimmed
  and chopped
50g (2oz) freshly grated coconut
sea salt

1 Heat the oil in a large frying pan, add the mustard seeds and fry until they start to pop, then add the urad dal and curry leaves. Cook, stirring, for 1–2 minutes or until the dal turns brown.

2 Add the onion and chillies and cook over a high heat for 1 minute, then lower the heat and cook for 5 minutes or until the onion is soft. Stir in the turmeric and a little salt.

3 Add the beans and cook, covered, for 15–20 minutes until tender. Stir in the grated coconut and serve.

The unique mild and nutty flavours of a thoran are derived from fried urad dal, curry leaves and freshly grated coconut, which is the most important ingredient.

Savoy cabbage and carrot thoran

Serves 4–6

2 green chillies, diced
2.5cm (1 inch) piece fresh ginger, peeled and chopped
3 garlic cloves, peeled
1 medium tomato, chopped
5 tbsp vegetable oil
1 tsp mustard seeds
1 tsp urad dal
2 onions, peeled and finely sliced
10 curry leaves
2 carrots, peeled and shredded
400g (14oz) Savoy cabbage, cored and shredded
200g (7oz) freshly grated coconut
sea salt

1 Using a pestle and mortar, grind the chillies with the ginger and garlic, then add the tomato and pound to make a paste.

2 Heat the oil in a large frying pan, add the mustard seeds and fry until they start to pop, then add the urad dal and cook, stirring, for 1–2 minutes or until the dal turns brown.

3 Add the onions together with the curry leaves and cook until soft. Add the chilli mixture and stir for 1 minute.

4 Add the shredded carrots, cabbage, 3 tbsp water and a little salt. Cover and cook for 10 minutes until the cabbage is just cooked. Stir in the grated coconut and cook for 2 minutes, then serve.

The thoran cooking technique suits most firm vegetables. It can also be applied to leafy greens – like cabbage – and starchy foods, such as cooked pulses, potato and plantain.

Okra masala

Illustrated on previous pages

Serves 4

3 tbsp vegetable oil
pinch of fenugreek seeds
pinch of fennel seeds
2–3 cardamom pods
2.5cm (1 inch) piece cinnamon stick
1 bay leaf
3 garlic cloves, peeled and chopped
3 onions, peeled and finely chopped
½ tsp ground turmeric
½ tsp chilli powder
1 tsp ground coriander
1 tsp tomato purée
2 tomatoes, finely chopped
200g (7oz) okra
coriander leaves, to serve

1 Heat the oil in a medium saucepan, karahi or wok. Add the fenugreek seeds, fennel seeds, cardamom pods, cinnamon stick, bay leaf, garlic and onions, and cook, stirring occasionally, for about 10 minutes until the onions are golden.

2 Add the turmeric, chilli powder, ground coriander and tomato purée, stir well and cook for a further minute. Add the chopped tomatoes and 600ml (1 pint) water, then bring to the boil and simmer for about 10 minutes until the sauce is thick.

3 In the meantime, top and tail the okra and cut into 1cm (½ inch) pieces. Stir the okra into the masala sauce, then cover and cook over a low heat for 5 minutes or until the okra is tender. Garnish with coriander leaves and serve with chapattis or toasted poppadoms.

Widely known as bhindi or ladies' fingers, okra is a favourite vegetable in India, prized for its flavour and texture. Choose relatively small okra as large ones tend to be stringy.

Aubergine stir-fry

Serves 4
4 tbsp vegetable oil
1 tsp mustard seeds
1 onion, peeled and thinly sliced
few curry leaves
1 green chilli, slit lengthways
500g (1lb 2oz) aubergines, cubed

1 Heat the oil in a large frying pan or wok. Add the mustard seeds and, when they start to pop, add the sliced onion and curry leaves and cook for 5 minutes or until the onion is soft.
2 Add the chilli and aubergine cubes and stir well. Cover and cook gently for 5 minutes, then remove the lid and stir-fry for 5 minutes or until the aubergines are tender. Serve hot.

Aubergine is considered a highly versatile vegetable in India and is available in an amazing array of colours, sizes and flavours. This is an easy way to enhance it, and uses just a few ingredients.

Green bean stir-fry

Serves 4

250g (9oz) green beans, trimmed
2 tbsp vegetable oil
1 tsp mustard seeds
2 onions, peeled and finely chopped
few curry leaves
3 green chillies, slit lengthways
large pinch of ground turmeric
sea salt

1 Cut the green beans into 2.5cm (1 inch) pieces. Heat the oil in a large frying pan or wok and fry the mustard seeds until they start to pop. Add the onions and curry leaves and cook for 4–5 minutes or until the onions are soft. Add the chillies, turmeric and a little salt and sauté for 1 minute.
2 Add the green beans, sprinkle in a few spoonfuls of water, then cover and cook for 5 minutes or until just tender. Remove the lid and stir-fry for 5 minutes or until the dish is dry and crunchy. Serve hot.

A speedy, light side dish such as this one is an excellent way to add a healthy component to a rich curry meal. You can use any variety of green bean – choose whichever looks freshest.

Green pepper stir-fry

Serves 4
300g (11oz) green peppers
4 tbsp vegetable oil
½ tsp cumin seeds
2 onions, peeled and finely sliced
2.5cm (1 inch) piece fresh root
   ginger, peeled and finely sliced

2 green chillies, slit lengthways
½ tsp ground turmeric
1 tsp ground coriander
2 tomatoes, finely chopped
2 tbsp finely chopped coriander
   leaves, to serve

1 Halve, core and deseed the green peppers, then slice finely into long strips.
Heat the oil in a large frying pan or wok. Add the cumin seeds, then the
onions, ginger and chillies. Cook, stirring occasionally, for 5 minutes or
until the onions are soft.
2 Add the turmeric and ground coriander and cook for a further minute
before adding the tomatoes. Stir well, then add the green peppers. Sprinkle
a few spoonfuls of water over the ingredients in the pan and cook for
5 minutes, stirring constantly, until the peppers are soft.
3 Transfer to a large serving dish, sprinkle with chopped coriander leaves
and serve hot.

Peppers bring a lot of colour to dishes,
whether they are used raw, grilled, or in a
stir-fry as they are here. This dish is an ideal
accompaniment to saucy curries.

Baby corn and carrot stir-fry

Serves 4

100g (3½oz) baby corn
100g (3½oz) baby carrots
2 tbsp vegetable oil
2 onions, peeled and sliced
   lengthways
2.5cm (1 inch) piece fresh root
   ginger, peeled and finely shredded
2 garlic cloves, peeled and chopped
½ tsp ground turmeric
½ tsp chilli powder
½ tsp garam masala
sea salt
2 tbsp chopped coriander leaves,
   to serve

1 Cut the baby corn lengthways into quarters. Halve the baby carrots lengthways. Set aside.

2 Heat the oil in a large frying pan. Add the onions, ginger and garlic, and cook, stirring occasionally, for 5 minutes or until the onions are softened and golden brown.

3 Add the turmeric, chilli powder and garam masala and cook, stirring, for a further minute. Stir in the baby corn and carrots, then sprinkle with a few spoonfuls of water and add a pinch of salt. Cook for 5 minutes, so that the vegetables are cooked, but still crunchy.

4 Remove the pan from the heat and scatter the coriander leaves over the stir-fry before serving.

Sweet baby vegetables combine to make the perfect crunchy vegetable side dish.

Spicy new potatoes with spinach

Illustrated on previous pages

Serves 4
350g (12oz) small or medium new
    potatoes
2 tsp ground turmeric
2 tbsp vegetable oil
1 tsp mustard seeds
1 tsp urad dal
1 green chilli, sliced

2.5cm (1 inch) piece fresh root
    ginger, peeled and finely chopped
1 large onion, peeled and chopped
1 tsp chilli powder
2 tomatoes, chopped
250g (9oz) baby leaf spinach
juice of ½ lemon
sea salt

1 Place the new potatoes in a large saucepan, cover generously with water and add ½ tsp turmeric and a little salt. Bring to the boil, cover and cook for 15 minutes or until the potatoes are tender. Drain and set aside.

2 Heat the oil in a large frying pan. Add the mustard seeds then, when they start to pop, add the urad dal, chilli and ginger, and stir-fry for 30 seconds. Add the onion and continue stir-frying until it is softened and light golden. Mix in the chilli powder, the remaining turmeric and a little salt, and stir-fry for a further minute.

3 Add the tomatoes and cook, stirring constantly, for 5 minutes or until they break down. Cover the pan and cook for a further 2 minutes, stirring the mixture frequently.

4 Add the spinach and cook, stirring constantly, for 5 minutes or until wilted. Lower the heat, add the drained potatoes and lemon juice and stir thoroughly to combine. Serve hot.

Spinach and coconut

Serves 4

100g (3½oz) freshly grated coconut
3 green chillies, chopped
4 tbsp vegetable oil
1 tsp mustard seeds
1 tsp urad dal
10 curry leaves
2 onions, peeled and finely chopped
1 tsp ground turmeric
300g (11oz) spinach leaves, chopped
sea salt

1 Place the grated coconut and chopped green chillies in a blender with 250ml (8fl oz) water and process to a coarse paste. Set aside.
2 Heat the oil in a medium saucepan or wok. Add the mustard seeds and, when they start to pop, add the urad dal and curry leaves. Stir-fry for 1–2 minutes or until the urad dal turns brown. Add the onions and stir-fry for 5 minutes or until soft.
3 Stir in the turmeric and a little salt and mix well, then add the chopped spinach leaves. Cover and cook for 5 minutes. Add the coconut paste and stir well. Lower the heat and cook gently for a further 5 minutes, stirring occasionally. Serve hot, with plain boiled rice and a simple moru curry (page 150) if you like.

You won't believe the difference freshly grated coconut and green chillies make to spinach. Use as much coconut as you like – the taste will only get better.

Stuffed peppers

Serves 6

3 peppers (red, yellow, orange)

For the stuffing

3 tbsp vegetable oil

½ tsp cumin seeds

2 garlic cloves, peeled and chopped

2 onions, peeled and finely chopped

¼ tsp ground turmeric

½ tsp chilli powder

½ tsp garam masala

150g (5oz) large white radishes,
 thinly sliced

150g canned chick peas, drained

2 tomatoes, finely chopped

2 tbsp chopped coriander leaves

sea salt

1 Preheat the oven to 200°C (fan oven 180°C), gas mark 6. Carefully slice off
the tops of the peppers and reserve to use as lids. Scrape out the seeds from
the pepper cavities. Oil a small baking dish that will hold the peppers
upright during baking, using 1 tbsp oil.

2 Heat 2 tbsp oil in a large frying pan, karahi or wok. Add the cumin seeds,
garlic and onions and fry for 5 minutes or until the onions are soft. Sprinkle
in the turmeric, chilli powder, garam masala and a little salt and stir well.

3 Add the radishes, chick peas and tomatoes, and cook for 5 minutes,
stirring frequently. Remove the pan from the heat and allow to cool slightly.

4 Fill the pepper cavities with the radish and chick pea mixture and replace
the tops. Place them upright in the oiled baking dish, sprinkle with 3 tbsp of
water and roast for 20 minutes or until the peppers are tender.

5 Carefully remove the lids from the peppers and scatter with chopped
coriander. Halve the peppers lengthways to serve.

I find the combination of peppery white radish
and sweet-tasting peppers excellent. For visual
appeal, use a selection of different coloured
peppers. The inclusion of chick peas make this
a substantial side dish.

indian pulses, cheese and eggs

Mung bean curry

Serves 4

150g (5oz) freshly grated coconut

2 green chillies

250g (9oz) mung beans

1 tsp chilli powder

½ tsp ground turmeric

2 potatoes, peeled and diced

4 tbsp vegetable oil

1 tsp mustard seeds

few curry leaves

3 dried red chillies

1 Place the coconut, green chillies and 250ml (8fl oz) water in a blender and process to a coarse paste. Set aside.

2 Put the mung beans in a saucepan with 750ml (1¼ pints) water. Add the chilli powder and turmeric and bring to the boil, then cover and cook for 20 minutes. Mix in the diced potatoes and continue simmering for a further 10–12 minutes or until the beans and potatoes are cooked.

3 Lower the heat and add the coconut and chilli paste. Stir well, then continue to simmer for a few minutes over a low heat.

4 Meanwhile, heat the oil in a small frying pan. Add the mustard seeds and, when they start to pop, add the curry leaves and the dried chillies. Pour the contents of the pan over the cooked mung beans, toss well and serve hot.

This dish is popular in Kerala at lunchtime. It is also served at breakfast with steamed rice cakes. You can vary this dish by using green bananas instead of potatoes.

Spinach and chick pea curry

Illustrated on previous pages

Serves 4

1 green chilli, deseeded and chopped
2.5cm (1 inch) piece fresh root
   ginger, peeled and finely chopped
2 tbsp vegetable oil
2 garlic cloves, peeled and sliced
1 onion, peeled and finely chopped
¼ tsp chilli powder
¼ tsp ground turmeric
½ tsp ground coriander
2 tsp tomato purée
400g (14oz) spinach leaves, tough
   stalks removed
410g can chick peas, drained and
   rinsed
sea salt

1 Using a pestle and mortar, finely grind the chilli and ginger together, adding a spoonful of water to help make a paste. Set aside.

2 Heat the oil in a large frying pan. Add the garlic and stir-fry for 30 seconds, then add the onion and cook, stirring constantly, for about 5 minutes until it is soft and lightly golden at the edges. Add the chilli powder, turmeric, ground coriander, chilli-ginger paste and tomato purée, and stir-fry for 2 minutes.

3 Pour 300ml (½ pint) water into the pan and bring to the boil. Stir in the spinach and chick peas, with a pinch of salt. Cook, stirring occasionally, for 5 minutes or until they are well blended with the spices and the spinach has wilted. Serve hot, with any Indian bread.

Chick peas are common in North India, where they are grown and available in an array of colours and shapes. The strong flavour of garam masala complements the chick peas well and spinach imparts colour and flavour.

Chick pea curry

Serves 4–6

4 tbsp vegetable oil
2.5cm (1 inch) piece cinnamon stick
2 cloves
3 cardamom pods, crushed
pinch of fennel seeds
4 garlic cloves, peeled and chopped
2.5cm (1 inch) piece fresh root
ginger, peeled and finely chopped
2 green chillies, finely chopped
3 onions, peeled and chopped
½ tsp ground turmeric

1 tsp chilli powder
1½ tsp ground coriander
½ tsp garam masala
1 tsp tomato purée
4 tomatoes, chopped
2 x 410g cans chick peas, drained
and rinsed
200ml (7fl oz) coconut milk
sea salt
4 tbsp chopped coriander leaves,
to serve

1 Heat the oil in a saucepan. Add the cinnamon stick, cloves, cardamoms, fennel seeds, garlic, ginger and chillies, and sauté for 1 minute. Add the onions and fry over a medium heat for 15–20 minutes or until they are soft and golden.

2 Add the turmeric, chilli powder, ground coriander, garam masala, tomato purée and salt. Mix well, then add the chopped tomatoes and 600ml (1 pint) water. Bring to the boil and add the chick peas. Cover and cook over a medium heat for 15 minutes, stirring occasionally.

3 Lower the heat and add the coconut milk. Simmer gently for 5 minutes or until the milk is well blended with the spices and chick peas. Remove the pan from the heat, scatter with chopped coriander leaves and serve hot.

This curry combines North and South Indian styles to create a unique taste. The strong spice blend married with the creamy texture of coconut milk makes it rather like a masala sauce. It is best served with a mild side dish.

Kidney bean curry

Serves 4–6

3 tbsp vegetable oil
1 tsp cumin seeds
5 garlic cloves, peeled and chopped
3 onions, peeled and sliced
2.5cm (1 inch) piece fresh root
 ginger, peeled and grated
1 tsp chilli powder
1 tsp ground coriander

1 tsp garam masala
½ tsp ground turmeric
5 tomatoes, chopped
410g can kidney beans, drained
 and rinsed
4 tbsp double cream
5 tbsp chopped coriander leaves,
 to serve

1 Heat the oil in a large saucepan. Add the cumin seeds and garlic, and cook briefly until the garlic is golden. Add the onions and ginger and cook, stirring occasionally, for about 10 minutes or until the onions are softened and golden.

2 Stir in the chilli powder, ground coriander, garam masala and turmeric. Add the tomatoes and kidney beans and cook, stirring constantly, for 1 minute. Pour in 400ml (14fl oz) water and bring the mixture to the boil. Lower the heat, cover and simmer gently for 20 minutes.

3 Remove the curry from the heat and stir in the cream. Scatter with chopped coriander leaves and serve with chapattis (page 236) or Malabar parathas (page 237).

Dried kidney beans are normally used for this dish, but I simmer canned beans with spices and tomato, enriching the curry with cream before serving. You could also add spinach to enhance the colour and flavour if you like.

Lentil and spinach dal

Serves 4–6

100g (3½oz) split red lentils
50g (2oz) mung beans
50g (2oz) chana dal, or yellow split
  peas
1 potato, peeled and chopped
3 onions, peeled and diced
3 green chillies, finely diced
3 tomatoes, chopped

1 tsp ground turmeric
1 tsp chilli powder
100g (3½oz) spinach leaves, tough
  stalks removed
4 tbsp vegetable oil
¼ tsp cumin seeds
3 garlic cloves, peeled and finely
  chopped

1 Put the split red lentils, mung beans and chana dal or yellow split peas in a saucepan. Add the potato, onions, chillies, tomatoes and ground spices, and stir well. Pour in 650ml (1 pint 2fl oz) water and bring to the boil.
2 Lower the heat, cover and simmer for 15 minutes or until the lentils are tender. Add the spinach leaves and cook for 5 minutes.
3 Heat the oil in a frying pan, add the cumin seeds and chopped garlic and sauté briefly. Pour this mixture over the dal to serve.

Dal is a delicious thick, soupy dish of lentils or other pulses. For many living on the Indian sub-continent, it is the most important dish they eat and an essential source of protein.

Red lentil dal

Serves 4–6

200g (7oz) split red lentils
2 onions, peeled and finely sliced
3 tomatoes, diced
4 garlic cloves. peeled and finely sliced
2.5cm (1 inch) piece fresh root ginger, peeled and finely diced
1 tsp chilli powder
1 tsp ground coriander
½ tsp ground turmeric
4 tbsp vegetable oil
1 tsp mustard seeds
10 curry leaves
sea salt

1 Put the split red lentils, onions, tomatoes, garlic, ginger, ground spices and a little salt into a saucepan. Pour in 1.2 litres (2 pints) water and bring to the boil.

2 Lower the heat, cover and simmer for 20 minutes or until the lentils are tender, then remove the lid and cook, uncovered, for a further 5 minutes.

3 Heat the oil in a frying pan, add the mustard seeds and fry until they pop, then add the curry leaves and sauté briefly. Pour this mixture over the dal to serve.

Mung bean and coconut dal

Serves 4–6
50g (2oz) freshly grated coconut
pinch of cumin seeds
200g (7oz) mung beans
2 green chillies, finely chopped

½ tsp ground turmeric
200ml (7fl oz) coconut milk
few curry leaves
sea salt

1 Put the freshly grated coconut and cumin seeds in a blender, add 250ml (8fl oz) water and whiz to a paste.
2 Put the mung beans in a saucepan with the chillies, turmeric, 1.2 litres (2 pints) water and a little salt. Bring to the boil, then lower the heat and simmer, covered, for 15 minutes or until the mung beans are tender.
3 Stir in the coconut paste and cook for 5 minutes. Lower the heat and add the coconut milk and a few curry leaves. Simmer for 5 minutes, then serve.

In India, different spices and lentils or other pulses are combined to give dals of varying thickness and smoothness – some mild and sweet, others hot in flavour.

Tarka dal

Serves 4–6
200g (7oz) split red lentils
50g (2oz) chana dal, or yellow split
  peas
2 onions, peeled and finely sliced
2 tomatoes, diced
2 garlic cloves, peeled and finely
  chopped
2 green chillies, finely sliced
1 tsp chilli powder
1 tsp ground turmeric
sea salt

To finish
2 tbsp vegetable oil
4 garlic cloves, peeled and shredded
½ tsp cumin seeds
chopped coriander leaves, to serve

1 Put the split red lentils, chana dal or yellow split peas into a saucepan and add the onions, tomatoes, chopped garlic, chillies, ground spices and a little salt. Pour in 1.5 litres (2½ pints) water and bring to the boil.
2 Lower the heat, cover and simmer for 20 minutes or until the lentils are tender, then remove the lid and cook, uncovered, for a further 5 minutes.
3 Heat the oil in a frying pan, add the shredded garlic and cumin seeds and sauté for 1 minute, then pour over the dal. Scatter over some chopped coriander leaves to serve.

Paneer with tomato and shallot chutney

Serves 2–4

150g (5oz) paneer cheese

vegetable oil, for deep-frying

For the chutney

3 tomatoes, roughly chopped

6 shallots, peeled and roughly
   chopped

1 green chilli, roughly chopped

2 tbsp coriander leaves

1 tbsp lemon juice

pinch of garam masala

sea salt

1 To make the chutney, put the tomatoes, shallots, chilli, coriander leaves and a little salt in a blender and process briefly until the tomatoes and shallots are just crushed. Transfer the mixture to a bowl and add the lemon juice and garam masala. Set aside.

2 Cut the paneer into large cubes. Heat the oil for deep-frying in a large, heavy-based saucepan, karahi or wok to 180°–190°C or until a cube of bread browns in 30 seconds. Deep-fry the paneer for 1–2 minutes or until lightly browned. Remove with a slotted spoon and drain on kitchen paper.

3 Serve the fried paneer hot or cold, with the tomato and shallot chutney spooned over the top.

I developed this dish to bring together the full flavour of paneer cheese with a refreshing shallot and tomato chutney.

Green pea and paneer cheese curry

Illustrated on previous pages

Serves 4

150g (5oz) paneer cheese
vegetable oil, for deep-frying
4 tbsp vegetable oil
3 small onions, peeled and sliced
2.5cm (1 inch) piece fresh root
   ginger, peeled and finely chopped
1 tsp ground coriander
½ tsp ground cumin

½ tsp ground turmeric
½ tsp garam masala
½ tsp poppy seeds
1 tsp tomato purée
100g (3½oz) peas
4 tbsp double cream
3 tbsp chopped coriander leaves
  (optional)
sea salt

1 Cut the paneer into 1cm (½ inch) cubes. Heat the oil for deep-frying in a large, heavy-based saucepan, karahi or wok to 180°–190°C or until a cube of bread browns in 30 seconds. Deep-fry the paneer cubes for 1–2 minutes or until golden, then remove with a slotted spoon and set aside to drain on kitchen paper.

2 Heat 4 tbsp oil in a saucepan, karahi or wok. Add the onions and ginger and cook, stirring occasionally, for 10 minutes until golden. Add the coriander, cumin, turmeric, garam masala and poppy seeds and cook for 2 minutes. Stir in the tomato purée and continue cooking for a further 3–4 minutes.

3 Pour in 250ml (8fl oz) water and bring the mixture to the boil. Simmer for 5 minutes, then add the peas, fried paneer and some salt and cook for a further 5 minutes.

4 Turn the heat as low as possible and stir in the cream. Cook gently for 2–3 minutes before adding the chopped coriander leaves if using. Serve hot, with a Malabar parathas (page 237) or other Indian flat bread.

Paneer dishes are now popular all over India, although they originated in the Punjab and other parts of North India. Paneer is an unusual cheese because it can be fried without a protective coating and stays firm, however, you must ensure that the oil is very hot so that the cheese colours quickly. Famously known as 'mutter paneer', this particular dish appears on most Indian restaurant menus.

Spinach and paneer

Serves 4

175ml (6fl oz) vegetable oil
50g (2oz) paneer cheese, cubed
½ tsp cumin seeds
4 garlic cloves, peeled and chopped
2 onions, peeled and diced
2 green chillies, finely chopped
5 curry leaves
250g (9oz) spinach leaves, finely
 chopped

1 tsp ground turmeric
1 tsp chilli powder
1 tsp garam masala
1 tsp ground coriander
2 tomatoes, finely chopped
1 green pepper, cored, deseeded
 and cubed
3½ tbsp single cream
125ml (4fl oz) milk
sea salt

1 Heat 125ml (4fl oz) oil in a deep frying pan. Add the paneer cubes and
cook, turning occasionally, for 1–2 minutes or until lightly browned all over.
Remove the pan from the heat, lift out the paneer cubes with a slotted spoon
and set aside to drain on kitchen paper.
2 Heat the remaining 4 tbsp oil in a large saucepan. Add the cumin seeds
and garlic and cook, stirring, for 1–2 minutes until golden. Add the onions,
chillies and curry leaves and cook, stirring occasionally, for 5 minutes or
until the onions are soft.
3 Add the spinach, turmeric, chilli powder, garam masala, ground coriander
and some salt. Mix well, then add the tomatoes and green pepper. Cook,
stirring from time to time, for 5 minutes or until the mixture is reduced
slightly and thick.
4 Stir in the cream and milk, then bring the mixture to the boil, stirring
constantly. Remove the pan from the heat, stir in the fried paneer and serve.

Crisp, chewy pieces of deep-fried paneer go
extraordinarily well with soft spiced spinach,
and the creamy texture of the sauce makes it
an ideal accompaniment to stronger dishes.

Egg curry

Serves 4

6 eggs
3 tbsp vegetable oil
1 tsp mustard seeds
2 garlic cloves, peeled and chopped
2 dried red chillies
10 curry leaves
1 onion, peeled and very finely sliced
1 tsp chilli powder

½ tsp ground coriander
½ tsp cumin seeds, crushed
½ tsp ground turmeric
1 tsp tomato purée
5 tomatoes, finely chopped
400ml (14fl oz) coconut milk
sea salt
2 tbsp chopped coriander leaves,
    to serve

1 Place the eggs in a large saucepan, cover with water and slowly bring to the boil, then lower the heat and simmer for 10 minutes. Drain and leave to cool in a bowl of cold water. Peel away the shells, rinse the eggs to remove any stray pieces, then set aside.

2 Heat the oil in a medium saucepan. Add the mustard seeds and, when they start to pop, add the garlic, dried chillies and curry leaves and sauté for 1 minute or until the garlic is golden. Add the onion with a good pinch of salt and cook, stirring constantly, for 5 minutes or until it is softened.

3 Stir in the chilli powder, ground coriander, crushed cumin and turmeric, then mix in the tomato purée and chopped tomatoes. Cook for 5 minutes, stirring constantly, until the sauce is well blended.

4 Lower the heat and pour in the coconut milk, stirring to combine. Gently drop the eggs into the sauce and cook gently for a further 5 minutes or until the eggs are hot and the sauce is thick. Scatter with chopped coriander leaves before serving.

Egg dishes are often made at home in India, especially in rural areas where people tend to keep chickens. Not only do eggs bring protein to meals, they are easy to cook and economical.

Egg and onion masala

Illustrated on previous pages

Serves 4

75g (3oz) freshly grated coconut
6 large eggs
3 tbsp vegetable oil
pinch of fennel seeds
pinch of fenugreek seeds
2 garlic cloves, peeled and finely
    chopped
2.5cm (1 inch) piece fresh root
    ginger, peeled and finely chopped

4 green chillies, slit lengthways
20 curry leaves
3 small onions, peeled and finely
    sliced
3 tomatoes, chopped
½ tsp ground turmeric
½ tsp chilli powder
sea salt
chopped coriander leaves, to serve

1 Place the grated coconut and 125ml (4fl oz) water in a blender and process until you have a fine paste. Set aside.

2 Place the eggs in a large saucepan, cover with water and slowly bring to the boil, then lower the heat and simmer for 10 minutes. Drain and leave to cool in a bowl of cold water. Peel away the shells, rinse the eggs to remove any stray pieces and set aside.

3 Heat the oil in a large saucepan. Add the fennel and fenugreek seeds and fry until they turn golden, then add the garlic, ginger, chillies and curry leaves and sauté for 2–3 minutes. Add the onions and fry for about 5 minutes until they are softened. Add the tomatoes, turmeric, chilli powder and a little salt and cook for 5 minutes or until the sauce is thick.

4 Lower the heat, stir in the coconut paste and cook for 5 minutes, stirring occasionally. Halve the hard-boiled eggs lengthways and add to the pan. Mix very gently until they are coated with the sauce. Warm through gently, then remove the pan from the heat.

5 Serve hot, scattered with chopped coriander. Accompany with rice or appams (page 242).

Indian scrambled eggs

Illustrated on previous pages

Serves 2
3 large eggs
2 tbsp vegetable oil
½ tsp mustard seeds
10 curry leaves
100g (3½oz) shallots, peeled and
 finely sliced

¼ tsp ground turmeric
¼ tsp chilli powder
1 tomato, chopped
sea salt
1 tbsp chopped coriander leaves,
 to serve (optional)

1 Break the eggs into a bowl and add a little salt. Whisk using a fork or hand whisk for 1–2 minutes or until well mixed and bubbles start to form on the surface.

2 Heat the oil in a large frying pan. Add the mustard seeds and, when they start to pop, add the curry leaves. Stir-fry for 2 minutes or until fragrant. Add the shallots and cook, stirring, over a low heat for about 5 minutes until softened.

3 Stir in the turmeric and chilli powder, then add the tomato and cook gently for 5 minutes. Pour in the beaten eggs and, using a wooden spoon, stir constantly for 3 minutes or so, until they are scrambled. Remove the pan from the heat and scatter lightly with chopped coriander if you like. Serve at once, with plain rice or bread.

This dish is essentially a thoran and in India it would be served as part of a meal. It is equally suitable for breakfast or brunch, served with bread or rice.

Spicy eggs with aubergine and spinach

Serves 4–6

6 eggs
4 tbsp vegetable oil
3 onions, peeled and sliced
   lengthways
3 green chillies, finely chopped
3 garlic cloves, peeled and finely
   chopped
2.5cm (1 inch) piece fresh root
   ginger, peeled and finely chopped
few curry leaves

1 tsp tomato purée
1 tsp ground coriander
½ tsp ground turmeric
½ tsp chilli powder
½ tsp garam masala
3 tomatoes, finely sliced
100g (3½oz) baby aubergines,
   quartered
100g (3½oz) baby spinach leaves
sea salt

1 Place the eggs in a large saucepan, cover with water and slowly bring to the boil, then lower the heat and simmer for 10 minutes. Drain and leave to cool in a bowl of cold water. Peel away the shells, rinse the eggs to remove any stray pieces and set aside.
2 Heat the oil in a frying pan or wok. Add the onions, chillies, garlic, ginger and curry leaves and cook, stirring frequently, for 5 minutes or until the onions are soft. Add the tomato purée, ground coriander, turmeric, chilli powder, garam masala and a little salt. Cook, stirring, for 1 minute.
3 Add the tomatoes, aubergines and spinach leaves. Cover and cook, stirring from time to time, for 6–7 minutes or until the sauce has blended well with the aubergines and spinach.
4 Add the hard-boiled eggs to the pan and allow them to heat through gently in the sauce for about 5 minutes before serving.

An ideal partner to this fiery egg dish would be Muslim-style rice with ghee (page 260), or even plain rice, and don't forget to have a cooling raita or some yogurt on the side.

indian
vegetables

Broccoli with panch phoron

Serves 4

3 tbsp vegetable oil
1 large onion, peeled and sliced
2.5cm (1 inch) piece fresh root
    ginger, peeled and shredded
2 dried red chillies, chopped
½ tsp ground turmeric
250g (9oz) broccoli, finely chopped
150g (5oz) white or green cabbage,
    finely sliced
1 tbsp ghee
sea salt

For the spice blend

2 tsp cumin seeds
2 tsp fennel seeds
2 tsp fenugreek seeds
2 tsp mustard seeds
2 tsp kalonji (nigella) seeds

1 To make the spice blend, put all the ingredients in a small spice mill and grind to a fine powder. Store in an airtight container.

2 Heat the oil in a large saucepan, karahi or wok. Add the onion and ginger and cook for 10 minutes or until golden. Add the chillies and turmeric, stir well, then add the broccoli, cabbage and a little salt. Sprinkle a few spoonfuls of water over the vegetable mixture and cover with a lid. Lower the heat and cook for 10 minutes or until the vegetables are tender.

3 Just before the vegetables are cooked, melt the ghee in a small frying pan. Add 1 tsp of the panch phoron spice blend, stir once, then quickly pour the contents of the frying pan over the broccoli mixture. Mix well and serve with chapattis (page 236) or other Indian bread.

Bengal in North-east India is known for its special 'panch phoron' spice blend. It is used mainly in vegetarian dishes to enhance flavour and create a pure Bengali aroma. It's easy to make and can be kept and used as required.

Sweet potato curry

Serves 4

400g (14oz) sweet potatoes, peeled
   and diced
3 green chillies
2.5cm (1 inch) piece fresh root
   ginger, peeled and thinly sliced
200ml (7fl oz) coconut milk
10 curry leaves
sea salt

1 Put the sweet potatoes in a large saucepan with the chillies and ginger. Add just enough water to cover and a pinch of salt. Bring to the boil, then simmer for about 10 minutes until the potatoes are tender.
2 Lower the heat and stir in the coconut milk and curry leaves. Simmer gently, stirring, for a few minutes to heat through, then serve.

A curry made from sweet potato is something unusual. Care must be taken to balance the spices with the sweetness of the vegetable, so follow the quantities precisely.

Cauliflower curry

Serves 4

3 tbsp vegetable oil
1 tsp fennel seeds
1 large onion, peeled and finely
  chopped
½ tsp ground turmeric
½ tsp chilli powder
4 tbsp tomato purée

250g (9oz) cauliflower florets
150g (5oz) green pepper, cored,
  deseeded and cubed
4 tomatoes, quartered
600ml (1 pint) milk
small bunch of coriander, finely
  chopped
sea salt

1 Heat the oil in a medium saucepan. Add the fennel seeds and cook, stirring constantly, for 1 minute or until golden brown. Add the onion and cook for 10 minutes, stirring frequently, until golden.
2 Add the turmeric and chilli powder and stir-fry for 2 minutes, then stir in the tomato purée. Add the cauliflower florets, green pepper, tomato quarters, milk, 250ml (8fl oz) water and some salt. Cook over a medium heat for 5–8 minutes, stirring constantly to prevent the milk splitting.
3 When the vegetables are tender, scatter with the chopped coriander and toss to mix. Serve with Malabar parathas (page 237) or cashew nut and lemon rice (page 258).

Cauliflower is very popular in North India, and this most typical dish, known as 'aloo gobi', is found on most restaurant menus.

Shallot and green banana theeyal

Illustrated on previous pages

Serves 4

2 green bananas or plantain, peeled

3 tbsp vegetable oil

250g (9oz) shallots, peeled and
 quartered

2 green chillies, slit lengthways

1 tsp ground turmeric

3 tomatoes, quartered

½ tsp mustard seeds

10 curry leaves

juice of 1 lime

sea salt

For the spiced coconut liquid

50g (2oz) freshly grated coconut

2 tbsp coriander seeds

3 dried red chillies

1 garlic clove, peeled

1 cinnamon stick

1 For the spiced coconut liquid, dry-toast all the ingredients in a large
frying pan for 4–5 minutes or until the coconut turns brown. Take the pan
off the heat and leave to cool for 5 minutes. Remove the cinnamon stick,
then transfer the mixture to a blender. Add 450ml (¾ pint) water and process
slowly until evenly blended.

2 Cut the bananas into 2.5cm (1 inch) pieces. Heat 2 tbsp oil in a large
saucepan or wok. Add the bananas, shallots and chillies and cook for
5 minutes or until the shallots are softened. Add the turmeric, coconut
liquid and a little salt, and cook over a medium heat, stirring occasionally,
for 5 minutes.

3 Mix in the tomatoes and cook over a low heat for 10 minutes or until the
shallots are very tender. When the curry is nearly ready, heat the remaining
1 tbsp oil in a frying pan. Add the mustard seeds and, when they start to
pop, add the curry leaves. Pour the contents of the frying pan over the curry
and stir through. Add the lime juice and cook over a medium heat for
3 minutes. Serve with plain rice and a little yogurt.

This dish is typical of the Nair community to which I belong and was a family favourite as I was growing up. It can be made with any chunky vegetable, but shallots are essential. You will find that it tastes even better the day after it is made.

Green paw paw curry

Serves 4

1 firm, unripe paw paw, about
    250g (9oz)
3 tbsp vegetable oil
1 tsp mustard seeds
pinch of fenugreek seeds
10 curry leaves, plus extra to
    garnish

3 dried red chillies
150g (5oz) shallots, peeled and finely
    chopped
2.5cm (1 inch) piece fresh root
    ginger, peeled and finely sliced
4 green chillies, slit lengthways
250ml (8fl oz) coconut milk
sea salt

1 Peel and chop the paw paw and place in a large saucepan. Cover
generously with water and add a little salt. Bring to the boil, then lower the
heat and simmer for 15 minutes or until the paw paw is tender. Drain and
set aside.

2 Heat the oil in a large saucepan or wok. Add the mustard seeds and, when
they start to pop, add the fenugreek seeds. Sauté for 1 minute or until the
seeds just turn golden. Add the curry leaves, dried chillies and shallots and
cook for 5 minutes or until the shallots are lightly golden.

3 Add the ginger, green chillies and a pinch of salt. Stir well, then add the
cooked paw paw and stir again. Turn the heat right down and slowly add
the coconut milk. Take the pan off the heat and stir the curry constantly for
2 minutes so that the coconut milk heats through gently.

4 Garnish with fresh curry leaves to serve. I like to eat this curry with plain
rice and sweet mango chutney (page 48).

In Indian cooking, fruit is often used in
savoury dishes as though it were a vegetable.
To achieve the right flavour and texture here,
the paw paw must be green and firm.

Courgette curry

Serves 4

3 tomatoes
2 garlic cloves, peeled
pinch of fennel seeds
3 tbsp vegetable oil
150g (5oz) shallots or onion, peeled
  and chopped
250g (9oz) courgettes, sliced
½ tsp ground turmeric
1 tsp chilli powder
300ml (½ pint) coconut milk

1 Put the tomatoes, garlic cloves and fennel seeds in a blender and process to make a rough paste, then set aside.
2 Heat the oil in a large saucepan or wok. Add the shallots and cook for 5 minutes or until soft. Add the courgettes, turmeric and chilli powder, and stir-fry for 5 minutes or until the courgettes are cooked but still crunchy.
3 Lower the heat and add the freshly ground tomato paste. Cook, stirring well, for 1 minute, then mix in the coconut milk. Bring to the boil, stirring, then lower the heat and simmer for 5 minutes. Serve hot, with rice or bread.

The courgette isn't an Indian vegetable, but I find it works well with Keralan spices. The refreshing taste of tomatoes with crushed fennel makes this a very different curry.

Vegetable and coconut milk stew

Illustrated on previous pages

Serves 4

1 tsp ghee or butter

12 shallots, peeled and cut into
   wedges

1½ tsp plain flour

3 tbsp tomato purée

½ tsp chilli powder

½ tsp ground coriander

½ tsp ground turmeric

250g (9oz) pumpkin, peeled and cut
   into batons

200g (7oz) green beans, trimmed

150g (5oz) cauliflower florets

100g (3½oz) peas

250ml (8fl oz) coconut milk

sea salt

1 Heat the ghee or butter in a large saucepan. Add the shallots and fry,
stirring, for 5 minutes or until golden. Remove from the heat and sprinkle
in the flour. Stir well and return to a low heat.

2 Slowly add 450ml (¾ pint) water, stirring well to prevent any lumps of
flour forming. Mix in the tomato purée, chilli powder, ground coriander and
turmeric, then add the pumpkin, green beans, cauliflower, peas and a little
salt. Cover and cook, stirring occasionally, for 20 minutes or until the
vegetables are tender.

3 Remove the pan from the heat and slowly pour in the coconut milk. Stir
constantly over a low heat for 2 minutes so that it heats through gently and
blends with the other ingredients. Serve immediately.

You can vary this mild dish, with whatever
fresh vegetables you have to hand.

Mixed vegetable masala

Serves 4

3 tbsp vegetable oil
2.5cm (1 inch) piece cinnamon stick
3 cloves
4–5 green cardamom pods, cracked
pinch of fennel seeds
5 shallots, peeled and very finely
  chopped
4 mixed sweet peppers (red, yellow
  orange, green)
4 tomatoes, quartered
3 potatoes, peeled and diced
3 carrots, peeled and diced
100g (3½oz) peas
2 tbsp chopped coriander leaves

For the spice paste

5 tbsp natural yogurt
1 tsp tomato purée
1 tsp chilli powder
½ tsp ground cumin
½ tsp ground turmeric
½ tsp garam masala

1 To make the spice paste, place the yogurt in a small bowl and stir in the tomato purée, chilli powder, cumin, turmeric and garam masala. Set aside.
2 Heat the oil in a large saucepan. Add the cinnamon, cloves, cardamom pods, fennel seeds and shallots and cook, stirring occasionally, for about 10 minutes until the shallots are soft and golden. Meanwhile, halve, core and deseed the peppers, then cut into dice.
3 Lower the heat under the pan, add the tomatoes and spicy yogurt paste and mix well. Pour in 600ml (1 pint) water and bring the mixture to the boil. Stir in the mixed peppers, potatoes, carrots and peas. Cover and cook for 10–15 minutes or until the vegetables are tender. Remove from the heat and scatter with chopped coriander leaves to serve.

You can use any selection of vegetables for this dish – try incorporating tropical varieties such as okra when they are available.

Sweet mango pachadi

Serves 4

200g (7oz) ripe mango
25g (1oz) jaggery or palm sugar
2.5cm (1 inch) piece fresh root
    ginger, peeled and finely sliced
½ tsp ground turmeric
3 tbsp vegetable oil
1 tsp mustard seeds
10 curry leaves
4 dried red chillies
sea salt

For the spice paste

75g (3oz) freshly grated coconut
2 green chillies
1 tsp mustard powder

1 For the spice paste, place all the ingredients in a blender and add 250ml (8fl oz) water. Process slowly to give a coarse paste.

2 Peel the mango and cut the flesh away from the stone, then cut into 2.5cm (1 inch) cubes. Place in a large saucepan and cover generously with water. Bring to the boil, then lower the heat and simmer for 5 minutes. Add the jaggery, ginger, turmeric and a little salt and simmer for a further 5 minutes or until the fruit is thoroughly cooked and the jaggery is well blended.

3 Add the coconut spice paste to the pan and stir to combine with the mango mixture, then lower the heat and cook gently for 5 minutes.

4 Just before it is ready, heat the oil in a small frying pan. Add the mustard seeds and, when they start to pop, add the curry leaves and dried chillies and cook for 1 minute. Pour the contents of the pan over the curry, stir to combine, then serve immediately.

Pachadi is a popular feast dish among Brahmins in South India, probably because its thick, creamy sauce offers a complete contrast to their usual spicy curries.

Garlic curry

Illustrated on previous pages

Serves 4

75g (3oz) tamarind pulp

3 tbsp vegetable oil

200g (7oz) garlic cloves, peeled

1 tsp fenugreek seeds

2 dried red chillies

½ tsp fennel seeds

10 curry leaves

3 onions, peeled and finely chopped

3 green chillies, slit lengthways

½ tsp ground turmeric

½ tsp chilli powder

2 tomatoes, finely chopped

1 Place the tamarind pulp in a small bowl and add 900ml (1½ pints) hot water. Break up the tamarind pulp as much as possible and set aside to soak for 20–30 minutes. Pass through a sieve into another bowl, pressing to extract as much tamarind flavour from the pulp as possible.

2 Heat 1 tbsp oil in a frying pan. Add 50g (2oz) garlic, ½ tsp fenugreek seeds and the dried chillies and fry for 1 minute. Remove with a slotted spoon and drain on kitchen paper. Transfer the cooked garlic and spices to a blender and process to a fine paste, then set aside.

3 Heat the remaining oil in a large frying pan. Add the fennel seeds and remaining fenugreek seeds and sauté for 1 minute or until they are brown. Add the curry leaves, onions and chillies. Cook over a medium heat for about 5 minutes until the onions are soft, then add the turmeric and chilli powder, followed by the tomatoes. Mix well and cook for 5 minutes, stirring often.

4 Stir in the remaining garlic cloves, the cooked garlic paste and the tamarind liquid. Lower the heat and cook gently, stirring frequently, for 15 minutes or until the mixture is thick and the garlic is well cooked. Serve with Malabar parathas (page 237).

People are always intrigued by this curry and the way the strong flavour of garlic is so well tamed by the spicy and tangy tamarind sauce.

Pumpkin curry

Serves 4

400g (14oz) yellow pumpkin
1 tsp ground turmeric
1 tsp chilli powder
200g (7oz) freshly grated coconut
½ tsp cumin seeds

3 tbsp vegetable oil
1 tsp mustard seeds
few curry leaves
2 dried red chillies
sea salt

1 Peel, deseed and cube the pumpkin, then place in a saucepan with the turmeric, chilli powder, a little salt and 600ml (1 pint) water. Bring to the boil, then simmer for 5 minutes or until well cooked.

2 Meanwhile, finely grind half of the coconut with the cumin seeds in a spice mill. Stir into the pumpkin mixture and cook for 2 minutes, stirring frequently. Take off the heat.

3 Heat the oil in a frying pan. Add the mustard seeds and, as they start to pop, add the curry leaves, dried chillies and the remaining coconut. Cook for about 4 minutes until the coconut is toasted. Tip the coconut mixture over the pumpkin curry, stir and serve. A simple moru curry (page 150) and plain rice are ideal accompaniments.

We grow a variety of pumpkins in South India and for each type there is a recipe that best highlights its unique texture and flavour. The use of roasted coconut is the distinguishing feature of this dish.

Green pea and pepper curry

Serves 4

3 tbsp vegetable oil

2.5cm (1 inch) piece fresh root ginger, peeled and grated

4 shallots, peeled and finely chopped

2 green chillies, slit lengthways

1 tsp ground coriander

1 tsp garam masala

½ tsp ground turmeric

½ tsp chilli powder

4 tomatoes, finely sliced

300g (11oz) peas

1 red pepper, cored, deseeded and chopped

1 tsp cracked black pepper

sea salt

2 tbsp finely chopped coriander leaves, to serve (optional)

1 Heat the oil in a large frying pan, karahi or wok. Add the grated ginger and sauté for a few seconds, then add the shallots and cook for 5 minutes or until they are soft.

2 Add the chillies, ground coriander, garam masala, turmeric and chilli powder, stir briefly, then add the sliced tomatoes and a little salt. Pour in 100ml (3½fl oz) water and mix well, then cover and cook for 5 minutes until the sauce is thick.

3 Lower the heat and add the peas and red pepper. Cook gently for about 10 minutes until the vegetables are tender. Stir in the cracked black pepper, then scatter with chopped coriander if you like. Serve hot, with Malabar parathas (page 237).

This tasty pea curry is made with a tomato and onion masala and an abundant flavouring of cracked black pepper.

Simple moru curry

Serves 4

1 tbsp vegetable oil
1 tsp mustard seeds
1 small onion, peeled and finely
sliced
2 dried red chillies
20 curry leaves

1cm (½ inch) piece fresh root ginger,
peeled and grated
1 green chilli, slit lengthways
1 tsp ground turmeric
400g (14oz) natural yogurt
sea salt

1 Heat the oil in a frying pan, add the mustard seeds and fry until they start
to pop. Add the onion, dried red chillies, curry leaves and 1 tsp salt. Cook
gently for 10 minutes or until the onion is softened and golden.
2 Add the grated ginger and green chilli, and cook, stirring, for 1 minute.
Stir in the turmeric and cook for 30 seconds.
3 Take off the heat and slowly stir in the yogurt, then heat gently for
1 minute, stirring constantly. Serve as a side dish, or with cashew nut and
lemon rice (page 258) or appams (page 242) as a simple meal.

No South Indian meal is complete without a
yogurt curry or 'moru kachiathu'. A thin,
smooth and vibrant yellow mixture of yogurt,
ginger and chillies, it enhances the foods it is
served with in an almost magical way.

Mixed pepper moru curry

Serves 4

4 tbsp vegetable oil

2 tsp mustard seeds

3 garlic cloves, peeled and finely chopped

3 dried red chillies

¼ tsp fenugreek seeds

10 curry leaves

2 onions, peeled and diced

3 green chillies, slit lengthways

2.5cm (1 inch) piece fresh root ginger, peeled and finely diced

150g (5oz) mixed red and yellow peppers

1 tomato, chopped

1 tsp ground turmeric

250g (9oz) natural yogurt

sea salt

1 Heat the oil in a frying pan, add the mustard seeds and fry until they start to pop. Add the garlic, dried red chillies, fenugreek seeds and curry leaves and cook for 2 minutes.

2 Add the onions, green chillies and ginger and cook gently for 10 minutes or until the onion is softened and golden. Meanwhile, halve, core and deseed the peppers, then cut into strips.

3 Stir the chopped tomato, turmeric and a little salt into the curry base, then add the mixed peppers and cook for 5 minutes.

4 Take off the heat and slowly stir in the yogurt. Heat gently for 1 minute, stirring, then serve.

When making moru, you must add the yogurt off the heat, stirring all the time, otherwise the mixture will curdle.

Spinach and mango moru curry

Serves 4

1 tbsp vegetable oil
1 tsp mustard seeds
1 small onion, peeled and finely
   sliced
20 curry leaves
2 dried red chillies
1cm (½ inch) piece fresh root ginger,
   peeled and grated

1 green chilli, slit lengthways
1 tsp ground turmeric
400g (14oz) natural yogurt
25g (1oz) spinach leaves, tough
   stalks removed
1 small mango, peeled and thinly
   sliced
sea salt

1 Heat the oil in a frying pan, add the mustard seeds and fry until they start to pop. Add the onion, curry leaves, dried red chillies and 1 tsp salt. Cook gently for 10 minutes or until the onion is softened and golden.
2 Add the grated ginger and green chilli, and cook, stirring, for 1 minute. Stir in the turmeric and cook for 30 seconds.
3 Take off the heat and slowly stir in the yogurt, then add the spinach and sliced mango. Heat gently, stirring, for 1 minute, then serve.

Vegetables or fruits may be added to a moru for a more substantial curry. Here the sourness of the yogurt provides a wonderful contrast to sweet mango.

Okra moru curry

Serves 4

150g (5oz) okra, sliced
6 tbsp vegetable oil
2 tsp mustard seeds
3 garlic cloves, peeled and finely
   chopped
3 dried red chillies
10 curry leaves
¼ tsp fenugreek seeds

2 onions, peeled and diced
3 green chillies, slit lengthways
2.5cm (1 inch) piece fresh root
   ginger, peeled and finely diced
1 tomato, chopped
1 tsp ground turmeric
250g (9oz) natural yogurt
sea salt

1 Top and tail the okra and cut into thin slices. Heat 2 tbsp oil in a frying
pan, add the okra and fry until crunchy. Remove and drain on kitchen
paper; set aside.
2 Heat the remaining oil in a clean frying pan, add the mustard seeds and
fry until they start to pop. Add the garlic, dried red chillies, curry leaves
and fenugreek seeds, and cook for 2 minutes.
3 Add the onions, green chillies and ginger, and cook for 10 minutes or
until the onion is softened and golden. Stir in the chopped tomato, turmeric
and salt, then add the okra and cook for 5 minutes.
4 Take off the heat and slowly stir in the yogurt, then return to a low heat
and warm gently, stirring, to serve.

indian
fish and
shellfish

Marinated sardines

Serves 2–3
450g (1lb) sardines, cleaned
4 tbsp vegetable oil
For the spice paste
2 tbsp lemon juice
2.5cm (1 inch) piece fresh root
   ginger, peeled and chopped

4 garlic cloves, peeled and crushed
1 tsp chilli powder
large pinch of ground turmeric
sea salt
To serve
lime wedges

1 First make the spice paste. Grind the lemon juice, ginger, garlic, chilli powder, turmeric and a little salt together to a fine paste, using a pestle and mortar or a small blender goblet.

2 Using a sharp knife, slash the sardines diagonally on both sides to allow the flavourings to permeate the flesh. Lay them side by side in a non-metallic dish, rub the spice paste all over and set aside to marinate for 10 minutes.

3 Heat the oil in a large frying pan and cook the sardines in batches if necessary. Place them in a single layer in the pan and fry over a low heat for about 2–3 minutes on each side until the skin is brown and crispy. Serve hot, with lime wedges.

Fish dishes are hugely popular in India's coastal states and this recipe is typical of Cochin, where it is eaten for lunch. Sardines work particularly well cooked in this way, but you can use other oily fish too.

Tuna and potato cutlets

Illustrated on previous pages

Makes 6–8

275g (10oz) tuna steaks, cubed

275g (10oz) potato, peeled and cubed

½ tsp ground turmeric, plus a pinch

2 tbsp vegetable oil

1 tsp mustard seeds

10 curry leaves

2.5cm (1 inch) piece fresh root ginger, peeled and chopped

1 green chilli, chopped

2 onions, peeled and chopped

½ tsp chilli powder

1 tsp garam masala

150g (5oz) cornflour

113g pack natural dried breadcrumbs

vegetable oil, for deep-frying

sea salt

1 Put the tuna, potato cubes, ½ tsp turmeric and a little salt in a saucepan. Add enough water to just cover and simmer until the potato is just cooked, about 15 minutes. Drain and transfer to a bowl.

2 Heat 2 tbsp oil in a large frying pan. Add the mustard seeds and, as they start to pop, add the curry leaves, ginger, chilli and onions and sauté for 5 minutes or until the onions are soft. Add the chilli powder, garam masala and pinch of turmeric. Cook gently for 2 minutes, stirring. Add to the tuna and potato and mash the mixture. Leave until cool enough to handle.

3 Divide the tuna mixture into 6–8 equal portions then, using wet hands, form into teardrop-shaped cutlets. Blend the cornflour with 200ml (7fl oz) water. Spread the breadcrumbs on a baking tray. Heat the oil for deep-frying in a suitable pan to 180°–190°C.

4 Dip each cutlet into the cornflour liquid, then coat with the breadcrumbs, pressing them on gently. Deep-fry in batches for 3–5 minutes until golden, turning frequently. Drain on kitchen paper and serve.

Tuna cutlets are often sold as a snack in Indian bakeries. They also make ideal party food if you shape the mixture into smaller patties. Serve them with a fresh chutney, or garlic and chilli pickle (page 43).

Fish steamed in banana leaves

Illustrated on previous pages

Serves 2–4
2 mackerel, each about 350g (12oz),
 cleaned and cut into 2.5cm
 (1 inch) slices
1 large banana leaf
For the spice paste
100g (3½oz) coriander leaves,
 chopped

1 onion, peeled and chopped
3 garlic cloves, peeled and chopped
1cm (½ inch) piece fresh root ginger,
 peeled and chopped
1 green chilli, chopped
½ tsp ground black pepper
2 tbsp lime juice
sea salt

1 To make the spice paste, place the chopped coriander, onion, garlic, ginger, chilli, black pepper and lime juice in a blender. Add a little salt and process to a smooth paste.
2 Transfer the spice paste to a large bowl, add the fish pieces and rub the paste carefully into the flesh. Set aside to marinate for 10 minutes.
3 Position a large steamer over a pan of water and bring to the boil. Dip the banana leaf briefly in a dish of hot water to soften and make it pliable, then shake gently to remove excess water and spread it out on a work surface.
4 Place the fish on the banana leaf, re-assembling it if you like, and spread the excess spice paste on top of the fish. Carefully wrap the leaf around the filling to make a parcel. Secure with string, strips of banana leaf, or small skewers. Place the parcel in the steamer and cook for 5–6 minutes.
5 To serve, lift the banana-wrapped fish on to a hot platter. Unwrap the parcel at the table so that everyone can savour the aroma.

Steaming allows you to enjoy the full flavour of the fish, and banana leaves add a special aroma. If you cannot find banana leaves, foil is a good alternative.

Lemon sole in tamarind sauce

Serves 6

50g (2oz) tamarind pulp
2 tbsp vegetable oil
1 tsp mustard seeds
10 curry leaves
pinch of fenugreek seeds
2 onions, peeled and chopped

¼ tsp ground turmeric
½ tsp chilli powder
1 tsp ground coriander
3 tomatoes, chopped
1 tsp tomato purée
600g (1¼lb) lemon sole fillets
sea salt

1 Place the tamarind pulp in a small heatproof bowl and break it up as much as possible. Add 100ml (3½fl oz) hot water and leave to soak for 20 minutes. Press the mixture through a sieve into a bowl and set aside, discarding the residue in the sieve.

2 Meanwhile, heat the oil in a large saucepan, karahi or wok. Add the mustard seeds and, when they start to pop, add the curry leaves and fenugreek seeds. Sauté for 1–2 minutes or until the fenugreek seeds turn brown. Stir in the onions and cook over a medium heat, stirring occasionally, for 10 minutes or until they are golden.

3 Add the turmeric, chilli powder and ground coriander, mix well, then add the chopped tomatoes, tomato purée and a little salt and cook for a further 2 minutes. Pour in the tamarind liquid and 200ml (7fl oz) water. Bring the mixture to the boil and simmer for 10–12 minutes, stirring occasionally, until the sauce thickens.

4 Cut the fish fillets into 2.5cm (1 inch) pieces and carefully mix into the sauce. Lower the heat and cook gently for 4–5 minutes or until the fish is just cooked through. Remove the pan from the heat and serve immediately.

This spicy, red-coloured dish has a distinctive and unforgettable flavour, thanks to the use of tamarind. In India, it would be cooked in a terracotta pot over a slow fire.

Lemon sole with coconut

Serves 6

2 tbsp vegetable oil
200g (7oz) shallots, peeled and
  chopped
10 curry leaves
600g (1¼lb) lemon sole fillets

For the spice paste

100g (3½oz) freshly grated coconut
1 tsp ground coriander
½ tsp chilli powder
large pinch of ground turmeric

1 To make the spice paste, place the coconut, ground coriander, chilli powder and turmeric in a blender. Pour in 200ml (7fl oz) water and process for 2–3 minutes to a smooth paste. Set aside.

2 Heat the oil in a large frying pan, karahi or wok. Add the shallots and curry leaves and cook over a medium-low heat for 5 minutes or until the shallots are soft. Stir in the coconut spice paste together with 100ml (3½fl oz) water and bring the mixture to the boil. Cook for about 5 minutes, stirring occasionally, until the sauce thickens.

3 Cut the fish fillets into 2.5cm (1 inch) pieces, add to the sauce and mix carefully. Cook gently for 4–5 minutes or until the fish is cooked through. Remove the pan from the heat and serve immediately.

The use of coconut milk in fish curries is typical of the inland areas of Kerala. Its smooth, creamy taste appeals to those who prefer mild curries. Other white fish can be used instead of lemon sole, if you prefer.

Salmon curry

Serves 4–6

1 tbsp tamarind pulp
2 tbsp vegetable oil
½ tsp mustard seeds
10 curry leaves
pinch of fenugreek seeds
1 large onion, peeled and chopped

½ tsp ground turmeric
½ tsp chilli powder
1 tsp ground coriander
2 tomatoes, chopped
500g (1lb 2oz) salmon fillet, cubed
200ml (7fl oz) coconut milk
sea salt

1 Place the tamarind pulp in a small heatproof bowl and cover with 3 tbsp hot water. Use a teaspoon to break up the tamarind as much as possible, then leave to soften for 15–20 minutes. Push the mixture through a sieve to extract 3 tbsp of tamarind-flavoured liquid, discarding any seeds and fibres.
2 Meanwhile, heat the oil in a large saucepan, karahi or wok. Add the mustard seeds and, when they start to pop, add the curry leaves and fenugreek seeds. Fry for 1 minute or until golden. Add the onion and cook over a medium-low heat for 10 minutes, stirring occasionally, until golden.
3 Add the turmeric, chilli powder and ground coriander and cook for a further minute. Add the tomatoes and a little salt and cook for 2 minutes, stirring constantly. Pour in the tamarind liquid and 300ml (½ pint) water and slowly bring to the boil.
4 Meanwhile, cut the salmon into 4cm (1½ inch) pieces. Lower the heat under the pan, add the fish cubes and simmer for 5–6 minutes or until the salmon is just cooked through.
5 Turn the heat as low as possible and pour in the coconut milk. Simmer gently for 2 minutes, then remove the pan from the heat. Serve immediately, with rice or potatoes.

This fish curry is popular in local village bars across India. Here I am using salmon, but of course in India it would be prepared with the local catch.

Fried fish in a spicy coriander batter

Serves 4

500g (1lb 2oz) white fish fillets, such
   as cod or haddock
vegetable oil, for deep-frying

For the batter

100g (3½oz) chick pea flour
50g (2oz) rice flour
1 tsp chilli powder
½ tsp garam masala
pinch of ground turmeric
1 green chilli, chopped
4 tbsp chopped coriander leaves
sea salt

1 To make the batter, put the flours, ground spices, green chilli, chopped coriander leaves and a little salt in a blender. Slowly blend in 200ml (7fl oz) water to make a smooth batter.

2 Cut the fish fillets into bite-sized pieces. Heat the oil in a deep-fryer, wok or large, heavy-based saucepan to 180–190°C or until a cube of bread dropped in browns in 30 seconds.

3 Dip the pieces of fish into the batter, then deep-fry in batches for about 1–2 minutes until golden. Drain on kitchen paper and serve at once, with sweet mango chutney (page 48) or a tomato chutney.

This is India's spicy take on fish and chips. It is a popular 'street food' snack.

Deep-fried prawns in spicy spinach batter

Illustrated on previous pages

Serves 4
500g (1lb 2oz) raw king prawns,
   peeled with tails left on
vegetable oil, for deep-frying
For the batter
100g (3½oz) chick pea flour
50g (2oz) rice flour
1 tsp chilli powder

½ tsp garam masala
pinch of ground turmeric
1 green chilli, chopped
20 curry leaves, finely chopped
50g (2oz) spinach leaves, stalks
   removed and finely chopped
sea salt

1 To make the batter, put the flours, ground spices, green chilli, chopped curry leaves, chopped spinach and a little salt in a blender. Slowly blend in 200ml (7fl oz) water to make a smooth batter.

2 Peel the prawns, leaving the tails on. Heat the oil in a deep-fryer, wok or large, heavy-based saucepan to 180–190°C or until a cube of bread dropped in browns in 30 seconds.

3 Dip the prawns into the batter to coat, then deep-fry in batches for about 1–2 minutes until crisp and golden. Drain on kitchen paper and serve immediately, with coconut chutney (page 46).

Deep-fried prawns in a spicy coconut batter

Serves 4

500g (1lb 2oz) raw king prawns, peeled with tails left on

vegetable oil, for deep-frying

For the batter

150g (5oz) cornflour

1 tsp chilli powder

¼ tsp ground turmeric

3 garlic cloves, peeled and finely chopped

2.5cm (1 inch) piece fresh root ginger, peeled and finely chopped

10 curry leaves, finely chopped

1 egg, beaten

100ml (3½fl oz) coconut milk

sea salt

1 To make the batter, put the cornflour, ground spices, garlic, ginger, chopped curry leaves and a little salt into a bowl. Make a well in the middle and add the egg and coconut milk. Mix to a smooth, thick batter.

2 Peel the prawns, leaving the tails on. Heat the oil in a deep-fryer, wok or large, heavy-based saucepan to 180–190°C or until a cube of bread dropped in browns in 30 seconds.

3 Dip the prawns into the batter to coat, then deep-fry in batches for about 1–2 minutes until crisp and golden. Drain on kitchen paper and serve plain or with sweet mango chutney (page 48).

Experiment with different fish and shellfish – try using squid rings instead of prawns here.

Prawn and mango curry

Serves 4–6

2 tbsp vegetable oil
½ tsp mustard seeds
10 curry leaves
2.5cm (1 inch) piece fresh root
    ginger, peeled and cut into
    julienne strips
2 green chillies, slit lengthways

2 large onions, peeled and sliced
1 unripened mango, peeled, stoned
    and cubed
½ tsp ground turmeric
400ml (14fl oz) coconut milk
500g (1lb 2oz) raw king prawns,
    peeled with tails left on
sea salt

1 Heat the oil in a large frying pan, karahi or wok. Add the mustard seeds and, when they start to pop, add the curry leaves, ginger, chillies and onions. Cook over a medium-low heat for 10 minutes, stirring occasionally, until the onions are golden.

2 Add the mango, turmeric and a little salt and mix well for 1 minute, then pour in the coconut milk and 200ml (7fl oz) water. Bring the mixture to the boil, stirring constantly.

3 Add the prawns to the pan and cook, stirring, for 5 minutes or until they turn pink and are cooked. Serve at once, with rice or appams (page 242).

In India, prawns are expensive and considered a luxury food, so a king prawn curry is enjoyed only on special occasions, or when prawns are sold cheaply in the market.

Prawn and tomato curry

Illustrated on previous pages

Serves 4–6

3 tbsp vegetable oil

pinch of cumin seeds

10 curry leaves

3 onions, peeled and sliced

½ tsp ground turmeric

1 tsp chilli powder

1 tsp tomato purée

4 tomatoes, sliced

500g (1lb 2oz) raw king prawns, peeled with tails left on

sea salt

chopped coriander leaves, to serve

1 Heat the oil in a large frying pan, karahi or wok. Add the cumin seeds, curry leaves and onions and cook over a medium-low heat for 10 minutes, stirring occasionally, until the onions are golden.

2 Add the turmeric, chilli powder, tomato purée, tomatoes and a little salt. Cook for 5 minutes, stirring constantly.

3 Add the prawns and cook for a further 5–6 minutes or until they turn pink and are cooked through.

4 Serve scattered with chopped coriander leaves on toasted poppadoms, or with adipoli parathas (page 240).

This authentic Keralan recipe has a thick consistency, making it a good alternative to the more usual saucy dishes.

Prawn stir-fry

Serves 4

400g (14oz) prawns (preferably raw), peeled

vegetable oil, for deep-frying

2 tbsp vegetable oil

½ tsp mustard seeds

10 curry leaves

100g (3½oz) shallots, peeled and sliced

½ tsp ground turmeric

½ tsp chilli powder

1 green chilli, slit lengthways

1 tbsp lemon juice

½ tsp ground black pepper

sea salt

1 Cut the prawns into 1cm (½ inch) pieces. Heat the oil for deep-frying in a large, heavy-based saucepan, karahi or wok to 180°–190°C or until a cube of bread browns in 30 seconds. Add the prawns and deep-fry until lightly golden; allow 45 seconds for cooked prawns; 1½ minutes for raw. Remove with a slotted spoon and set aside to drain on kitchen paper.

2 Heat 2 tbsp oil in a large frying pan, karahi or wok. Add the mustard seeds and, when they start to pop, add the curry leaves and sliced shallots. Cook, stirring, for 5 minutes or until the shallots are soft. Stir in the turmeric, chilli powder, green chilli and some salt. Cook, stirring, for a further 2 minutes.

3 Add the prawns and stir-fry over a medium-low heat for 5 minutes. Pour in the lemon juice, then stir in the black pepper, remove the pan from the heat and serve immediately.

This delicious prawn dish, enriched with lots of curry leaves and shallots, is easy to make at home and full of crunchy fresh flavours.

Prawns with toasted coconut sauce

Serves 4–6
3 tbsp vegetable oil
½ tsp mustard seeds
10 curry leaves
1 large onion, peeled and chopped
½ tsp ground turmeric
½ tsp chilli powder
2 tomatoes, quartered
500g (1lb 2oz) raw prawns, peeled

50ml (2fl oz) coconut milk
2 tbsp lime juice
sea salt
For the spice paste
2 tbsp coriander seeds
100g (3½oz) freshly grated coconut
10 curry leaves
1 dried red chilli

1 To make the spice paste, place all the ingredients in a dry frying pan and toast over a medium-low heat, stirring constantly, for 5 minutes or until the coconut turns brown. Set aside to cool.

2 Transfer the toasted coconut mixture to a blender or food processor and process, gradually adding 300ml (½ pint) water to make a thin, smooth paste. Set aside.

3 Heat the oil in a large saucepan, karahi or wok. Add the mustard seeds and, when they start to pop, add the curry leaves and onion. Cook for 10 minutes, stirring occasionally, until the onion is light golden. Add the turmeric, chilli powder, tomatoes and a little salt and cook, stirring, for 2 minutes.

4 Pour in the coconut paste, then increase the heat and bring the mixture to the boil. Add the prawns and simmer for 5 minutes or until they turn pink and are cooked. Lower the heat, stir in the coconut milk and simmer gently for 2 minutes. Remove the pan from the heat and stir in the lime juice.

5 Serve with adipoli parathas (page 240) and a thoran (pages 66–70).

Pepper-fried crab

Illustrated on previous pages

Serves 2–4
1 medium cooked crab, about 450g
   (1lb), cleaned
2 tbsp ghee
1cm (½ inch) piece fresh root ginger,
   peeled and crushed
2 garlic cloves, peeled and crushed
10 curry leaves
1 large red onion, peeled and sliced
½ tsp ground turmeric
1 green chilli, finely sliced
2 tomatoes, cut into wedges
3 tbsp lemon juice
1 tsp ground black pepper
sea salt

1 Using a strong knife, halve or quarter the crab. Make sure that the small
stomach sac behind the mouth and the inedible, feathery grey gills ('dead
man's fingers') are removed.
2 Heat the ghee in a large frying pan, karahi or wok. Add the ginger, garlic,
curry leaves and onion and stir-fry over a medium-low heat for 3 minutes.
3 Add the turmeric, sliced chilli, tomato wedges and some salt to the pan
and continue stir-frying for a further 2 minutes.
4 Increase the heat slightly, then add the crab pieces and stir-fry for
2 minutes. Lower the heat, add the lemon juice and black pepper and cook
gently for a further 3 minutes. Serve immediately.

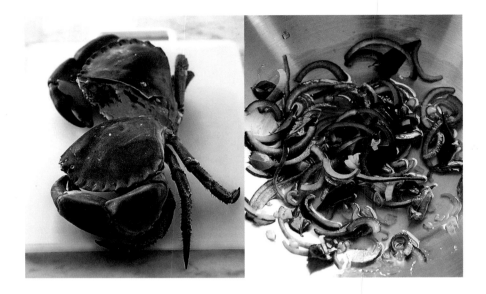

If you want to eat crab, this is the way to do it: make a mess with the shell and thoroughly enjoy it. Some say this is the best crab dish they have ever tasted – try it!

Crab thoran

Serves 4

2 tbsp vegetable oil
½ tsp mustard seeds
10 curry leaves
3 garlic cloves, peeled and chopped
2.5cm (1 inch) piece fresh root
    ginger, peeled and finely chopped

2 large onions, peeled and chopped
150g (5oz) coconut, freshly grated
½ tsp ground turmeric
½ tsp chilli powder
½ tsp ground black pepper
400g (14oz) cooked white crabmeat
sea salt

1 Heat the oil in a large frying pan, karahi or wok. Add the mustard seeds and, when they start to pop, add the curry leaves, garlic, ginger and onions. Cook over a medium-low heat, stirring occasionally, for 5 minutes or until the onions are soft.

2 Add the grated coconut, turmeric, chilli powder, black pepper and a little salt and stir-fry for 2 minutes. Increase the heat slightly, then add the crabmeat and continue stir-frying for a further 4–5 minutes. Serve at once.

Fresh coconut gives this simple recipe a lovely light texture. It is a dry dish that can be eaten on its own or as a side dish. It also works well with prawns.

Curried mussels

Serves 2–4
450g (1lb) fresh mussels
2 tbsp vegetable oil
½ tsp cumin seeds
1 bay leaf
5 garlic cloves, peeled and finely
  chopped

2 onions, peeled and finely chopped
½ tsp ground turmeric, plus a large
  pinch
2 tomatoes, finely chopped
2 tbsp lime juice
2 tbsp chopped coriander leaves
sea salt

1 Clean the mussels by scrubbing the shells under cold running water and removing any beards that are attached to them. Discard any with cracked or broken shells, or any that refuse to close when tapped sharply with a knife. Set the prepared mussels aside.

2 Heat the oil in a large frying pan. Add the cumin seeds, bay leaf, garlic and onions and fry for about 5 minutes until the onions are soft. Add ½ tsp turmeric, a pinch of salt and the tomatoes. Cook over a low heat, stirring well, for 3 minutes.

3 Meanwhile, put the mussels in a large saucepan with a large pinch of turmeric and a little salt. Add cold water to cover and bring to the boil. Simmer for 2–3 minutes or until the mussels have steamed opened. Discard any that do not open.

4 Quickly drain the mussels, reserving the cooking liquid. Add the mussels to the onion mixture and cook, stirring, for 2 minutes. If you would like the sauce to be thinner, add some of the reserved mussel cooking water. Add the lime juice and scatter in the chopped coriander leaves. Remove the pan from the heat and serve immediately.

indian poultry and meat

Marinated chicken with hot pepper sauce

Serves 4

4 chicken portions (quarters or breasts)

4 garlic cloves, peeled and chopped

2.5cm (1 inch) piece fresh root ginger, peeled and sliced

3 tbsp vegetable oil

10 curry leaves

2 onions, peeled and finely chopped

2 tsp ground coriander

½ tsp chilli powder

½ tsp ground turmeric

2 tomatoes, chopped

1 tsp ground black pepper

For the spice paste

1 tsp garam masala

½ tsp ground turmeric

sea salt

1 To make the spice paste, mix the garam masala, turmeric and a little salt with about 2 tbsp water in a small bowl. Place the chicken portions in a shallow, non-metallic dish and spread the paste all over them. Set aside to marinate for 10 minutes.

2 Meanwhile, using a pestle and mortar or small spice mill, grind the garlic and ginger together to make a paste. Set aside.

3 Heat the oil in a saucepan, karahi or wok. Add the curry leaves and onions and fry for 2 minutes, then add the garlic-ginger paste and cook, stirring occasionally, for 5 minutes or until the onions are soft. Add the ground coriander, chilli powder and turmeric, stir well, then add the tomatoes and a little salt. Cook gently for 1–2 minutes.

4 Lay the marinated chicken portions in the pan, spooning some of the onion mixture over the top. Pour in 600ml (1 pint) water and bring to a simmer. Cook for 20–25 minutes or until the chicken is cooked through. Stir in the black pepper, cook for a further 2 minutes, then serve hot.

The Andhra Pradesh region is well known for its fiery dishes that use a variety of chillies. Here is a moderately hot version of a popular local dish.

Chicken with roasted coconut sauce

Illustrated on previous pages

Serves 4

500g (1lb 2oz) skinless chicken
   thigh fillets
3 tbsp vegetable oil
½ tsp mustard seeds
10 curry leaves
2 onions, peeled and finely sliced
2 tomatoes, chopped
½ tsp ground turmeric
sea salt

For the spice paste

1 tbsp vegetable oil
100g (3½oz) freshly grated coconut
2 bay leaves
1 cinnamon stick
½ tsp ground black pepper
2 cloves
1 tsp ground coriander
½ tsp chilli powder

1 To make the spice paste, heat the oil in a frying pan. Add the coconut, bay
leaves, cinnamon, black pepper and cloves and toast, stirring constantly, for
3–5 minutes or until the coconut is golden.
2 Take off the heat and stir in the ground coriander and chilli powder.
Discard the cinnamon stick. Tip into a blender, pour in 400ml (14fl oz) water
and process for 3–5 minutes to a fine paste. Set aside.
3 Cut the chicken into thick strips and set aside. Heat 3 tbsp oil in a large
saucepan, karahi or wok. Add the mustard seeds and, when they start to
pop, add the curry leaves and onions. Cook, stirring frequently, for
5 minutes or until the onions are soft.
4 Add the tomatoes, turmeric and a little salt and stir-fry for 2 minutes. Add
the chicken strips, coconut paste and 600ml (1 pint) water and bring to a
simmer. Cook gently for 15–20 minutes or until the chicken is cooked
through. Serve hot.

There is nothing quite like the wonderful aroma of freshly roasted coconut. The ingredients in this recipe are beautifully balanced and the resulting dish has a lovely colour and natural creamy coconut flavour.

Home-style chicken

Illustrated on previous page

Serves 4

3 tbsp vegetable oil
2.5cm (1 inch) piece cinnamon
   stick
2 bay leaves
3 cloves
2 onions, peeled and chopped
10 curry leaves
1 tbsp ground coriander
1 tsp garam masala
½ tsp ground turmeric
½ tsp chilli powder
2 tomatoes, finely chopped
500g (1lb 2oz) skinless chicken
   thigh fillets, cubed, or 750g
   (1lb 10oz) chicken pieces on
   the bone
sea salt
2 tbsp chopped coriander leaves,
   to serve

1 Heat the oil in a large saucepan or flameproof casserole. Add the cinnamon stick, bay leaves and cloves and cook for 1–2 minutes or until fragrant. Add the onions and curry leaves and cook, stirring occasionally, for 5 minutes or until the onions are soft.
2 Stir in the ground coriander, garam masala, turmeric and chilli powder, then the tomatoes and a little salt. Cook for 5 minutes, stirring occasionally.
3 Add the chicken, mix well, then pour in 350ml (12fl oz) water. Bring to a simmer and cook gently for 15 minutes or until the chicken is cooked through. Serve scattered with the coriander leaves.

Known as 'kozhy curry', this dish is quick and simple, and uses ingredients that are easy to find. Boneless chicken thighs are convenient, but using chicken on the bone will give the sauce a richer flavour.

Bengali chicken curry

Serves 4–6

500g (1lb 2oz) skinless chicken
  thigh or breast fillets, cubed
¼ tsp ground turmeric
4 tbsp vegetable oil
sea salt
3 tbsp coriander leaves, finely
  chopped, to serve

For the spice paste

6 shallots, peeled and chopped
2 green chillies, chopped
3 garlic cloves, peeled
2.5cm (1 inch) piece fresh root
  ginger, peeled and chopped
1 tsp ground mustard seeds
½ tsp ground turmeric

1 For the spice paste, place all the ingredients in a blender and process, adding a few spoonfuls of water to make a smooth. thick paste.

2 Place the chicken in a non-metallic bowl. In another bowl, mix together the turmeric, a pinch of salt and a tiny amount of water to make a smooth paste. Rub this mixture all over the chicken and set aside for 5–10 minutes or so.

3 Heat 2 tbsp oil in a large frying pan or wok. Add the chicken and stir-fry over a medium heat for 10 minutes or until it is golden. Remove the pan from the heat and set aside.

4 Heat the remaining oil in another large saucepan. Add the spice paste and fry over a low heat for 2 minutes, then add the chicken and cook gently, stirring well, for 3–4 minutes. Pour in 300ml (½ pint) water, cover the pan and simmer gently over a medium heat for 15 minutes or until the chicken is cooked through. Scatter with chopped coriander leaves and serve hot.

This recipe was given to me by a friend from Calcutta, when I expressed my interest in the Bengalis' unique style of cooking.

Duck curry

Serves 4–6

5 tbsp vegetable oil
¼ tsp fennel seeds
pinch of fenugreek seeds
2 large onions, peeled and sliced
2 green chillies, chopped
2.5cm (1 inch) piece fresh root
  ginger, peeled and finely shredded
1 tsp ground turmeric
½ tsp chilli powder
450g (1lb) duck breast, cubed
200g (7oz) baby new potatoes, halved
  if large
5 tbsp wine vinegar or cider vinegar
400ml (14fl oz) coconut milk
few curry leaves, or to taste
sea salt

1 Heat the oil in a large saucepan. Add the fennel and fenugreek seeds and stir-fry for 30 seconds. Add the onions, chillies and ginger to the pan and fry over a medium heat for 5 minutes or until the onions are soft.
2 Sprinkle in the turmeric, chilli powder and a little salt. Mix well, then add the duck and new potatoes, stir well and stir-fry for 10 minutes or until lightly browned.
3 Pour in the vinegar, then stir in 200ml (7fl oz) coconut milk and 250ml (8fl oz) water. Lower the heat to medium-low, cover and cook gently for 20 minutes, stirring occasionally.
4 When the duck is tender and the potatoes are well cooked, turn the heat right down and pour in the remaining 200ml (7fl oz) coconut milk, stirring to combine. Gently mix in the curry leaves, then remove the pan from the heat and serve the curry hot.

Duck is not a typical ingredient for most Indian people, but in Kerala, our beautiful backwater region has lots of ducks and they feature in several dishes.

Chicken or duck tikka

Serves 4
500g (1lb 2oz) skinless chicken
or duck breast fillets, cut into 2.5cm
  (1 inch) cubes
For the tikka marinade
2.5cm (1 inch) piece fresh root
  ginger, peeled and chopped
3 garlic cloves, peeled

225g (8oz) natural yogurt
1 tbsp lime juice
1 tbsp chopped coriander leaves
½ tsp chilli powder
¼ tsp ground turmeric
large pinch of garam masala
sea salt

1 To prepare the tikka marinade, using a pestle and mortar, grind the ginger and garlic together to make a smooth paste. Transfer to a bowl and add the yogurt, lime juice, chopped coriander leaves, chilli powder, turmeric, garam masala and salt to taste. Whisk together until smooth.
2 Put the chicken or duck into a non-metallic dish and rub the tikka marinade thickly and evenly over the pieces. Cover and leave to marinate for 15–20 minutes.
3 Preheat the grill or barbecue. Thread the marinated chicken or duck on to 4 metal skewers or pre-soaked wooden skewers. Place on the grill (or barbecue) rack and cook for 5–10 minutes, turning frequently, until browned on all sides. Serve at once, with a salad if you like.

The marinated and grilled dishes known as tikka are traditionally cooked in an Indian tandoor oven. It isn't possible to create the same intense, dry heat of a tandoor at home, but grilling still produces delicious results.

Chicken tikka masala

Serves 4

500g (1lb 2oz) skinless chicken
breast fillets, cut into 2.5cm (1 inch)
cubes

For the tikka marinade

2.5cm (1 inch) piece fresh root
ginger, peeled and finely chopped
3 garlic cloves, peeled
225g (8oz) natural yogurt
1 tbsp lime juice
1 tbsp chopped coriander leaves
½ tsp chilli powder
¼ tsp ground turmeric
large pinch of garam masala
sea salt

For the masala

2.5cm (1 inch) piece fresh root
ginger, peeled and finely chopped
4 garlic cloves, peeled
4 tbsp vegetable oil
1 large onion, peeled and chopped
½ tsp ground turmeric
½ tsp chilli powder
1 tsp ground coriander
1 tsp tomato purée
200g (7oz) tomatoes, chopped
1 green pepper, cored, deseeded and
finely chopped
4 tbsp double cream

To serve

¼ tsp garam masala
2 tbsp chopped coriander leaves

1 To prepare the tikka marinade, using a pestle and mortar, grind the
ginger and garlic together to make a smooth paste. Transfer to a bowl and
add the yogurt, lime juice, chopped coriander leaves, chilli powder, turmeric,
garam masala and salt to taste. Whisk together until smooth.
2 Put the chicken into a non-metallic dish and rub thickly and evenly with
the tikka marinade. Cover and leave to marinate for 15–20 minutes.
3 For the masala, using a pestle and mortar, grind the ginger and garlic
together to make a smooth paste. Heat the oil in a saucepan, add the onion
and sauté for 10 minutes until soft. Add the ginger-garlic paste and sauté
for 2 minutes. Stir in the turmeric, chilli powder and ground coriander.
Add the tomato purée, chopped tomatoes and green pepper and sauté for
2 minutes. Pour in 350ml (12fl oz) water and bring to the boil, then lower
the heat and cook, covered, for 20–25 minutes until thickened.
4 Preheat the grill. Place the chicken pieces on the grill rack and cook,
turning, until lightly charred and cooked through.
5 When the masala sauce is thick, lower the heat and pour in the cream. Add
the grilled chicken and season with salt to taste. Heat through for a few
minutes. Serve sprinkled with garam masala and chopped coriander leaves.

Pork vindaloo

Serves 6–8

900g (2lb) boneless pork, cubed

4 tbsp vegetable oil

3 garlic cloves, peeled and chopped

2 onions, peeled and sliced

1 tsp ground turmeric

½ tsp chilli powder

1 tsp tomato purée

3 tomatoes, chopped

3 tbsp wine or cider vinegar

sea salt

coriander leaves, to serve

For the spice paste

1 tsp cumin seeds

4 dried red chillies

4 cardamom pods

4 cloves

2.5cm (1 inch) piece cinnamon stick

10 black peppercorns

2.5cm (1 inch) piece fresh root
    ginger, peeled and chopped

4 garlic cloves, peeled

3 tbsp wine or cider vinegar

1 To make the spice paste, put the cumin seeds, dried chillies, cardamom pods, cloves, cinnamon and peppercorns in a small spice mill and grind to a fine powder. Transfer the mixture to a blender, add the ginger, garlic and vinegar and process to a smooth paste.

2 Place the pork in a large, non-metallic bowl, add the spice paste and stir to coat well. Cover with cling film and set aside to marinate in a cool place for 1½ hours.

3 Heat the oil in a large saucepan or flameproof casserole. Add the garlic and sauté for 1 minute. Add the onions and cook gently for 10–15 minutes, stirring occasionally, until the onions are golden.

4 Add the turmeric, chilli powder, tomato purée, chopped tomatoes and vinegar. Mix well, then add the marinated pork and a little salt and cook, stirring constantly, for 10 minutes.

5 Pour in 275ml (9fl oz) water and bring the mixture to the boil. Lower the heat, cover and simmer gently for 30 minutes or until the meat is cooked through and the sauce is thick. Serve hot, scattered with coriander leaves.

Vindaloo is a very traditional dish from Goa, though pork dishes are not common elsewhere in India. Use beef, lamb, chicken or prawns, if you prefer.

Lamb tikka with naan

Serves 4
500g (1lb 2oz) boneless lamb, cut
   into 2.5cm (1 inch) cubes
For the tikka marinade
2.5cm (1 inch) piece fresh root
   ginger, peeled and chopped
3 garlic cloves, peeled
225g (8oz) natural yogurt
1 tbsp lime juice
1 tbsp chopped coriander leaves
½ tsp chilli powder
¼ tsp ground turmeric
large pinch of garam masala
sea salt
To serve
4 naan breads
lime wedges

1 To prepare the tikka marinade, using a pestle and mortar, grind the ginger and garlic together to make a smooth paste. Transfer to a bowl and add the yogurt, lime juice, chopped coriander leaves, chilli powder, turmeric, garam masala and salt to taste. Whisk together until smooth.
2 Put the lamb into a non-metallic dish and rub thickly and evenly with the tikka marinade. Cover and leave to marinate for 15–20 minutes.
3 Preheat the grill or barbecue. Thread the marinated lamb on to four metal skewers or pre-soaked wooden skewers. Place on the grill (or barbecue) rack and cook for 10 minutes, turning until browned and crunchy on all sides.
4 Meanwhile, sprinkle the naan breads with water and grill or bake according to the packet instructions. Serve the tikka with the naan and lime wedges. Accompany with a tomato, cucumber and onion salad, and coconut chutney (page 46) or sweet mango chutney (page 48).

Lamb korma

Illustrated on previous pages

Serves 4–6

2.5cm (1 inch) piece fresh root
ginger, peeled and chopped
4 garlic cloves, peeled
3 tbsp vegetable oil
2.5cm (1 inch) piece cinnamon stick
3 cloves
2 bay leaves
3 cardamom pods, crushed
pinch of fennel seeds
2 onions, peeled and chopped

1 tsp ground coriander
¼ tsp ground turmeric
½ tsp chilli powder
2 tsp tomato purée
500g (1lb 2oz) boneless lamb, cubed
pinch of ground black pepper
40g (1½oz) cashew nuts
1 tbsp coriander leaves
handful of toasted cashew nuts, to
serve

1 Using a pestle and mortar, grind the ginger and garlic together to make a
fine paste; set aside. Heat the oil in a saucepan, karahi or wok. Add the
cinnamon stick, cloves, bay leaves, cardamom, fennel seeds and onions and
sauté for 5 minutes or until the onions are soft.
2 Add the ginger-garlic paste, then the ground coriander, turmeric, chilli
powder and tomato purée. Mix well and cook over a low heat for 5 minutes,
stirring occasionally. Stir in the lamb and pepper and pour in 150ml (¼ pint)
water. Cover and simmer gently for 30 minutes or until the lamb is tender.
3 Meanwhile, using a pestle and mortar, grind the cashew nuts with a little
water to make a smooth paste. When the lamb is cooked, add the cashew nut
paste and stir well. Simmer for 3 minutes, then remove from the heat and
serve scattered with coriander leaves and toasted cashew nuts.

Many people think of korma as a 'safe' dish to order because of its mild taste, but in India it's not only mildness that's important – a creamy texture is essential too. In this case it's created with a paste made from cashew nuts. The same method can be applied to other meat and poultry. You may like to serve the korma with yogurt and a sprinkling of garam masala.

Lamb with coconut slivers

Serves 4–6

2.5cm (1 inch) piece fresh root
   ginger, peeled and sliced
3 garlic cloves, peeled and chopped
2.5cm (1 inch) piece cinnamon stick
2 bay leaves
3 cloves
20 curry leaves
5 tbsp vegetable oil
2 onions, peeled and finely chopped
1 tbsp ground coriander
½ tsp ground turmeric
½ tsp chilli powder
100g (3½oz) coconut, shaved into
   slivers
500g (1lb 2oz) boneless lamb, cubed
½ tsp mustard seeds
2 green chillies, slit lengthways

1 Using a small spice mill or pestle and mortar, grind the ginger, garlic, cinnamon stick, bay leaves, cloves and 10 curry leaves together. Set aside.
2 Heat 3 tbsp oil in a large saucepan, karahi or wok. Add the onions and fry, stirring occasionally, for 5 minutes or until soft. Add the freshly ground spice mixture, the ground coriander, turmeric, chilli powder, coconut slivers and 400ml (14fl oz) water. Bring the mixture to the boil, then add the lamb cubes. Lower the heat and simmer gently for 30 minutes or until the lamb is well cooked.
3 Heat the remaining oil in a separate small frying pan. Add the mustard seeds and, when they start to pop, add the remaining 10 curry leaves and the chillies. Stir-fry for 1 minute, then add the contents of the pan to the cooked meat and continue cooking. stirring frequently, for about 10 minutes or until the lamb mixture is very dry.
4 Serve hot, with naan or other Indian bread.

People are fascinated by the spicy flavour of this dish, and the stronger the better, if you can handle it. Beef can be used in place of the lamb, if you prefer.

Lamb and potato curry

Serves 4–6

5 tbsp vegetable oil

2.5cm (1 inch) piece fresh root
ginger, peeled and chopped

4 garlic cloves, peeled and chopped

2 green chillies, chopped

15 curry leaves

2 onions, peeled and sliced

2 tsp ground coriander

½ tsp ground turmeric

½ tsp chilli powder

3 tomatoes, sliced

400g (14oz) boneless lamb, cubed

200g (7oz) baby new potatoes,
scrubbed

1 tsp mustard seeds

1 Heat 4 tbsp oil in a saucepan. Add the ginger, garlic, chillies and 5 curry leaves and sauté for 3 minutes or until the ginger and garlic are golden brown. Add the onions and cook, stirring frequently, for 10 minutes until lightly browned.

2 Stir in the ground coriander, turmeric and chilli powder, mix well, then add the tomatoes, lamb and 400ml (14fl oz) water. Bring to a simmer and cook over a low heat for 15 minutes.

3 Stir in the new potatoes and continue cooking for 15 minutes or until the lamb is cooked and the potatoes are tender.

4 Meanwhile, heat the remaining 1 tbsp oil in a small frying pan. Add the mustard seeds and, when they start to pop, add the remaining 10 curry leaves and stir well. Pour the contents of the frying pan over the lamb mixture, stir briefly, then remove the pan from the heat.

5 Serve with Malabar parathas (page 237), or other Indian bread.

You can use beef rather than lamb for this curry, if you prefer.

Rogan josh

Serves 4

5 tbsp vegetable oil

2 bay leaves

1 red onion, peeled and chopped

400g (14oz) boneless lamb, cubed

5 tbsp ground almonds

sea salt

For the spice paste

500g (1lb 2oz) natural yogurt

2.5cm (1 inch) piece fresh root
 ginger, peeled and chopped

2 tsp garam masala

1 tsp chilli powder

½ tsp fennel seeds

large pinch of ground cardamom

1 To make the spice paste, place all the ingredients in a blender and process until smooth. Set aside.

2 Heat the oil in a large saucepan. Add the bay leaves and red onion and sauté over a medium heat for 2 minutes.

3 Add the lamb and stir-fry for 5 minutes or until the meat is evenly browned. Slowly add the spice paste, stirring constantly to help the meat absorb the essence of the paste. Reduce the heat to low, cover and cook gently for 30 minutes or until the lamb is tender.

4 Add the ground almonds and salt to taste. Serve hot with Malabar parathas (page 237).

Almonds are a speciality of Kashmir and many parts of Northern India. Although more common in sweet dishes, they are a traditional feature of this richly flavoured lamb curry.

Stir-fried dry beef curry

Serves 4–6

500g (1lb 2oz) silverside beef, cubed
½ tsp ground turmeric
½ tsp chilli powder
3 tbsp vegetable oil
5 garlic cloves, peeled and chopped

1 large onion, peeled and sliced
1½ tsp ground coriander
1 tsp ground black pepper
1 tsp garam masala
20 curry leaves
sea salt

1 Place the beef, turmeric and chilli powder in a large saucepan or casserole. Pour in 400ml (14fl oz) water and bring to a simmer, then cover and cook gently for 30 minutes or until the beef is tender. Add salt to taste, then remove the pan from the heat and set aside.

2 Shortly before the beef has finished simmering, heat the oil in a large frying pan, karahi or wok. Add the garlic and sauté until it is brown, then add the onion and cook, stirring occasionally, for 10 minutes or until golden. Sprinkle in the ground coriander and sauté for 2 minutes.

3 Drain the excess liquid from the cooked beef mixture, then transfer the meat to the pan of spicy onions. Add the black pepper, garam masala and curry leaves and cook, stirring, over a medium heat for 10 minutes until the mixture is very dry.

4 Serve with appams (page 242) and a moru curry (page 150) if you like.

This dry curry is very different from the more usual saucy curries, as the cooked beef should be dry enough to pick up with your fingers. Feel free to make this dish hotter and spicier.

indian breads and rice

Pooris

Makes 6
200g (7oz) plain flour, plus extra to
   dust
½ tbsp vegetable oil
vegetable oil, for deep-frying
sea salt

1 Place the flour in a large bowl with a generous pinch of salt. Gradually stir in the oil, then about 100ml (3½fl oz) water or just enough to make a smooth dough. Cover and set aside for 10 minutes.

2 Knead the dough on a lightly floured work surface for 2–3 minutes. Divide the dough into 6 equal portions, about the size of a golf ball. Roll each ball out as thinly as possible to make a neat round.

3 Heat the oil for deep-frying in a deep-fryer, wok or large, heavy-based saucepan to 180–190°C or until a cube of bread browns in 30 seconds. At the same time, place a cast-iron griddle or a large, heavy-based frying pan over a high heat to heat thoroughly.

4 One at a time, toast the rounds of dough on the hot, unoiled griddle pan for 30 seconds on each side. Then, using a spatula or fish slice, transfer the poori to the hot oil and deep-fry for about 2 minutes, turning constantly, to help it puff up. Remove from the pan and drain on kitchen paper while you toast and deep-fry the remaining dough rounds. Serve immediately.

These light, puffy pooris are easy to make, look appetising and taste good. They are excellent with vegetable masala curries, and with chicken and lamb dishes.

Chapattis

Makes 8
400g (14oz) wholemeal flour, plus
   extra to dust
2 tsp vegetable oil
sea salt

1 Place the flour and a pinch of salt in a large bowl. Gradually stir in the oil, then mix in about 200ml (7fl oz) water to make a smooth dough.
2 Knead the dough on a lightly floured work surface for about 3 minutes, then divide the mixture into 8 equal portions, about the size of a golf ball. Working one at a time, roll out the balls of dough as thinly as possible, turning them frequently to make an even round.
3 Heat a flat cast-iron griddle pan or large, heavy-based frying pan. When thoroughly hot, cook the chapattis in batches as necessary. Place on the griddle pan and toast for 1–2 minutes each side or until the dough is cooked and very lightly speckled, turning them frequently. Remove and keep warm while you cook the remaining chapattis. Serve immediately.

The majority of Indian people eat chapattis at most meals, serving them with curries or even simply a pickle. They are the most popular of all Indian breads, and will complement most of the savoury dishes in this book.

Malabar parathas

Makes 4

125g (4oz) wholemeal flour, plus
   extra to dust
2 tbsp vegetable oil, plus extra to oil

1 Place the flour in a large bowl. Gradually stir in the vegetable oil and
about 150ml (¼ pint) water or just enough to make a soft dough. Knead the
dough on a work surface for 3–4 minutes, then return to the bowl, cover and
set aside to rest for 1 hour.
2 Divide the dough into 4 equal portions. Keeping the unused portions
covered to prevent them drying out, take one piece of dough and roll it into
a ball, then dust lightly with flour.
3 On a clean work surface or board, roll out the dough to a round, about
15cm (6 inches) in diameter, and brush the top lightly with a thin layer of
vegetable oil. Roll up the dough to make a long, thin cigar shape, then
carefully place one end of the dough in the middle of your palm and wind
the rest around and around to make a coil.
4 Flatten the coiled dough with the palms of your hands and dust with flour.
Return it to the work surface and carefully roll it out into a 12cm (5 inch)
round. Cover and set aside while you repeat the process with the remaining
balls of dough.
5 Place a flat cast-iron griddle pan over a medium-high heat for about
10 minutes until very hot. Place 1–2 parathas on it and sprinkle with a little
oil. Cook, turning frequently, for about 2–3 minutes on each side or until
golden and cooked. Keep warm while you cook the rest, then serve warm.

This rich-tasting South Indian flat bread is an
excellent accompaniment to Kerala's light
vegetable curries. It is a flaky bread that pulls
apart temptingly in mouthwatering layers.

Adipoli parathas

Makes 8

225 g (8oz) wholemeal flour, plus
  extra to dust
4 tbsp vegetable oil, plus extra to
  brush

For the prawn filling

8 tbsp vegetable oil
½ tsp mustard seeds
1 green chilli, chopped
2.5cm (1 inch) piece fresh root
  ginger, peeled and grated
2 onions, peeled and finely chopped
10 curry leaves
½ tsp ground turmeric
150g (5oz) raw prawns, peeled
2 eggs, beaten
sea salt

1 To make the dough, place the wholemeal flour in a large bowl. Gradually stir in the oil and about 150ml (¼ pint) water to make a soft, pliable dough. Knead on a work surface for 3–4 minutes, then return to the bowl, cover and set aside for 1 hour.

2 To make the filling, heat the oil in a frying pan. Add the mustard seeds and, when they start to pop, add the chilli, ginger, onions and curry leaves. Cook over a medium-low heat for 5 minutes, stirring occasionally, until the onions are soft. Add the turmeric and a little salt and sauté for 1 minute. Add the prawns and cook for 7–10 minutes, stirring occasionally, until they have turned pink and are cooked. Remove from the heat and set aside.

3 Divide the dough into 8 equal portions. Place one piece in the palm of your hands and roll it into a smooth ball. Lightly dust with flour, then place it on a board and roll out as thinly as possible, to make a paper-thin round, about 22cm (8½ inches) in diameter.

4 Heat a flat cast-iron griddle or large, heavy-based frying pan. Brush with oil and, when hot, add a round of dough. Stir the eggs into the prawn mixture, then spread 3 tbsp of this filling on top of the dough on the griddle pan. Cook over a medium heat for 5 minutes or until browned underneath.

5 Lower the heat, then carefully turn the paratha over with a spatula and cook for a further 5 minutes or until the prawn mixture is well stuck to the paratha. Turn it over again and transfer the paratha to a board. Roll the paratha into a cylinder shape to enclose the prawn mixture. Repeat with the remaining dough and filling. Cut each stuffed paratha in half to serve.

Appams

Makes 4–6
250g (9oz) basmati rice
125g (4oz) freshly grated coconut
1 tsp sugar
1 tsp fast-action dried yeast
75g (3oz) semolina
sea salt
a little oil, for cooking

1 To make the batter, wash the basmati rice in plenty of cold water, then place in a bowl, add fresh cold water to cover and leave to soak for 1 hour. Drain, reserving 225ml (7½fl oz) water. Put the rice and reserved water in a blender and process to a batter. Add the freshly grated coconut and whiz until fairly smooth; set aside.

2 In a bowl, dissolve the sugar in 5 tsp warm water, then add the dried yeast, cover and set aside. Put the semolina and 100ml (3½fl oz) water in a saucepan over a medium heat and cook, stirring, for 15 minutes or until thick.

3 Transfer to a bowl, add the rice batter and yeast mix, stir well and cover with a damp cloth. Set aside for 4 hours or until the batter is bubbly and doubled in volume. Stir in 1 tsp salt, carefully to avoid knocking air out of the batter.

4 To cook the appams, heat an oiled griddle pan or non-stick frying pan. Add a ladleful of batter and spread out thinly to make a large pancake. Cover and cook for 2 minutes on one side only, so the top remains moist; carefully remove to a warm plate. Repeat to make 4–6 appams.

5 Serve warm, as a snack with a fresh chutney, or as an accompaniment.

These soft, spongy pancakes, made from fermented white rice, are a typical dish of the Keralan Christian community. They are traditionally served with lamb stew, although they also provide a contrast to spicier dishes.

Onion masala appams

Illustrated on previous pages

Makes 4–6
250g (9oz) basmati rice
125g (4oz) freshly grated coconut
1 tsp sugar
1 tsp fast-action dried yeast
75g (3oz) semolina
sea salt
a little oil, for cooking

For the onion topping
2 tbsp vegetable oil
½ tsp mustard seeds
10 curry leaves
1 red onion, peeled and chopped
1 green chilli, finely sliced

1 Make the batter as for basic appams (page 242).
2 Heat the oil in a frying pan, add the mustard seeds and, as they start to pop, add the curry leaves and red onion and cook for 5 minutes. Add the green chilli and cook for a further 2 minutes.
3 Heat an oiled griddle or non-stick frying pan. Add a ladleful of the appam batter and spread out thinly to make a large pancake. Cover and cook for 2 minutes on one side only, so the top remains moist. Gently spread 1 tbsp of the onion mixture on top. Carefully turn the pancake over and cook for about 3 minutes until the onion is golden and embedded in the batter. Carefully invert on to a warm plate. Repeat to make 4–6 appams.
4 Serve warm, as a snack with a fresh chutney, or as an accompaniment.

Egg appams

Makes 4–6
250g (9oz) basmati rice
125g (4oz) freshly grated coconut
1 tsp sugar
1 tsp fast-action dried yeast
75g (3oz) semolina
sea salt
a little oil, for cooking
4–6 eggs

1 Make the batter as for basic appams (page 242).
2 Heat an oiled griddle or non-stick frying pan. Add a ladleful of batter and spread thinly to make a large pancake. Cover and cook for 2 minutes.
3 Remove the lid and crack an egg into the middle of the appam. Re-cover and cook for further 2–3 minutes or until the base is golden and crisp and the egg is lightly cooked.
4 Transfer the appam to a plate and serve immediately. Repeat to make 4–6 appams, using all the batter and eggs.

These appams are delicious served as a brunch or breakfast. Prepare the batter a day ahead and keep chilled once it has fermented.

Sweet appams

Makes 4–6

250g (9oz) basmati rice
125g (4oz) freshly grated coconut
1 tsp sugar
1 tsp fast-action dried yeast
75g (3oz) semolina
sea salt
a little oil, for cooking

For the sweet topping

4 tbsp thin honey
4 tbsp palm sugar, grated (or an
    extra 2 tbsp honey)
freshly grated coconut, to serve
    (optional)

1 Make the batter as for basic appams (page 242).
2 Just before cooking, warm the honey and mix with the palm sugar, if using; set aside.
3 Heat an oiled griddle or non-stick frying pan. Add a ladleful of batter and spread out thinly to make a large pancake. Cover and cook for 2 minutes on one side only, so the top remains moist. Carefully remove to a warm plate. Repeat to make 4–6 appams.
4 Serve hot, drizzled with the honey mixture and sprinkled with grated coconut if desired.

This is my favourite way to eat appams. They are perfect for breakfast and if you haven't any freshly grated coconut to hand, simply drizzle with a little coconut milk instead.

Vermicelli and rice

Serves 4

3 tbsp ghee
100g (3½oz) vermicelli
2 tbsp vegetable oil
½ tsp mustard seeds
1 tsp urad dal
10 curry leaves
25g (1oz) cashew nuts

2 green chillies, finely chopped
2.5cm (1 inch) piece fresh root
    ginger, peeled and grated
50g (2oz) freshly grated coconut
100g (3½oz) white rice, cooked
sea salt
2 tbsp chopped coriander, plus
    a few whole leaves, to serve

1 Heat the ghee in a large frying pan over a medium heat. When hot, add the vermicelli and stir-fry for 5–6 minutes or until golden. Remove with a slotted spoon and set aside to drain on kitchen paper.

2 Heat the oil in another frying pan. Add the mustard seeds, urad dal, curry leaves and cashew nuts and fry for 1–2 minutes or until the nuts and urad dal turn brown. Add the chillies, ginger and a little salt, then pour in 400ml (14fl oz) water and bring to the boil. Lower the heat, add the vermicelli and simmer for 3–4 minutes until thoroughly blended with the spices.

3 Add the grated coconut and cooked rice. Carefully mix with the vermicelli and allow to warm through briefly. Transfer to a serving bowl, scatter with coriander and serve.

Tempered spices give this rice and noodle dish a wonderful flavour. Serve as an alternative to plain rice, as a complete meal.

This is a variation of a colourful rice dish often served with an array of dishes at special functions in India. Personally, I find it is delicious eaten on its own with a simple raita. The use of ghee gives it a special richness.

Vegetable rice

Illustrated on previous pages

Serves 4–6

2 green chillies

2.5cm (1 inch) piece fresh root
  ginger, peeled and chopped

2 garlic cloves, peeled

400g (14oz) white basmati rice

4 tbsp vegetable oil

½ tsp cumin seeds

1 cinnamon stick

5 cardamom pods

10 curry leaves

2 onions, peeled and finely chopped

½ tsp ground turmeric

1 tsp chilli powder

3 tomatoes, chopped

100g (3½oz) potato, peeled and diced

100g (3½oz) cauliflower florets

75g (3oz) peas

2 tbsp ghee

sea salt

2 tbsp chopped coriander leaves,
  to serve

1 Using a small spice mill or pestle and mortar, grind the chillies, ginger
and garlic together to make a fine paste. Set aside. Wash the rice in plenty of
cold water and set aside to drain thoroughly.

2 Heat the oil in a large saucepan. Add the cumin seeds, cinnamon,
cardamom pods and curry leaves and sauté for 1 minute, then add the
onions and cook over a medium heat for 5 minutes, stirring occasionally.
Add the fresh chilli paste and cook for a further 5 minutes or until the
onions are golden. Add the turmeric, chilli powder, tomatoes and a little salt,
and cook for 1 minute, stirring occasionally.

3 Add the rice, potato, cauliflower, peas and ghee and fry for 2 minutes.
Pour in enough hot water to cover and give it a good stir. Bring to the boil,
then lower the heat and simmer for 20 minutes or until the rice and
vegetables are cooked.

4 Transfer to a serving dish and scatter with chopped coriander to serve.

Cashew nut and lemon rice

Illustrated on previous pages

Serves 4

200g (7oz) white long-grain or
  basmati rice
½ tsp ground turmeric
juice of ½ lemon
2 tbsp vegetable oil
1 tsp mustard seeds
2 dried red chillies
1 tsp chana dal or urad dal
3–5 curry leaves, plus extra to
  garnish
50g (2oz) cashew nuts
sea salt

1 Wash the rice in plenty of cold water, then drain and place in a large, heavy-based saucepan. Add 750ml (1¼ pints) water, the turmeric and a little salt. Stir well and bring to the boil over a high heat. Lower the heat slightly and simmer for 20 minutes or until the rice is cooked. Drain thoroughly and return to the saucepan. Stir in the lemon juice and set aside in a warm place.
2 Heat the oil in a small frying pan. Add the mustard seeds and, when they start to pop, add the dried red chillies, chana dal, curry leaves and cashew nuts. Stir-fry for 2–3 minutes or until the dal and cashew nuts are lightly browned, then pour the contents of the frying pan over the lemon rice.
3 Transfer the rice to a serving dish and garnish with a few extra curry leaves. Serve immediately as an alternative to plain boiled rice, or with a moru curry (pages 150–5) and a thoran (pages 66–70) as a complete meal.

With its fresh citrus flavour and the fragrance of curry leaves, this lemon rice is exceptional. Cashew nuts give the dish a richer taste and chana dal adds its own nutty flavour.

Muslim-style rice with ghee

Serves 4–5

250g (9oz) basmati rice

6 tbsp ghee

50g (2oz) cashew nuts

1 tbsp raisins

5 cardamom pods, lightly crushed

1 large onion, peeled and chopped

sea salt

1 Wash the basmati rice thoroughly in plenty of cold water, then drain and set aside in a sieve to drain thoroughly.

2 Heat the ghee in a large saucepan. Add the cashew nuts, raisins and cardamom pods and fry for 2–3 minutes until the cashews turn golden. Add the onion and cook, stirring frequently, for 5 minutes or until it is soft and lightly golden.

3 Stir in the drained rice and stir-fry for 5 minutes or until the rice grains are translucent. Add 1 litre (1¾ pints) water and a little salt. Bring to the boil, then lower the heat, cover the saucepan and cook gently for 20 minutes or until the rice is tender and all the water has been absorbed. Serve hot.

Biryani and similar richly flavoured rice dishes are specialities of India's Muslim communities. This simple, yet delicious rice preparation is served with spicy meat dishes in the Malabar region of Kerala.

Boiled rice

Serves 4

200g (7oz) white basmati or other
  long-grain white rice
sea salt

1 Wash the rice in plenty of cold water, then drain and place in a large, heavy-based saucepan. Add 750ml (1¼ pints) fresh water and a little salt and stir well. Place the saucepan over a high heat and bring to the boil. Lower the heat slightly and simmer for 20 minutes or until the rice is cooked. Drain thoroughly and serve hot.

Rice is a key part of any Indian meal and in North India basmati rice is very popular because of its pure white colour, clean flavour and exotic fragrance.

indian
desserts
and drinks

Rasa fruit salad

Serves 4–6

1 small pineapple
1 large wedge of watermelon
100g (3½oz) seedless green grapes, halved
100g (3½oz) seedless red grapes, halved
2 oranges
1 seedless guava or mango
100ml (3½fl oz) mango juice
100ml (3½fl oz) passion fruit juice
5 tbsp lime juice
20g (¾oz) mint leaves, shredded

1 Cut away the skin from the pineapple, remove the 'eyes', then quarter, core and cut the flesh into chunks. Place the pineapple in a large salad bowl. Remove the skin and seeds from the watermelon, then cut into chunks. Add to the pineapple together with the grapes.

2 Peel the oranges, removing all white pith, then cut out the segments between the membranes and add to the prepared fruit. Peel and chop the guava or mango and add to the bowl.

3 Pour the mango and passion fruit juices over the fruits. Add the lime juice, toss gently and scatter over the shredded mint leaves. Serve in individual dishes, with a scoop of coconut or vanilla ice cream if you like.

This fruit salad is a fantastic blend of various fruits and juices, and the perfect finish to a lovely meal.

In India we make a number of desserts from
carrots, including halwa which is from the
North. In South India, milky puddings like
this one are more popular. These are prepared
with different fruits, grains and nuts.

Carrot pudding

Illustrated on previous pages

Serves 4
1.2 litres (2 pints) milk
pinch of powdered saffron
250g (9oz) carrots, peeled
3 tbsp ghee
150g (5oz) caster sugar
50g (2oz) pistachio nuts, skinned
25g (1oz) blanched almonds,
    chopped
1 tsp ground cardamom
extra pistachio nuts and almonds,
    shredded, to serve (optional)

1 Pour 3 tbsp of the milk into a small bowl, add the saffron and set aside to
infuse for 5–10 minutes until the milk is orange in colour. Slowly bring the
remaining milk to the boil in a large saucepan, then simmer over a medium
heat for 10 minutes. Lower the heat and continue to simmer, stirring, for
20 minutes.
2 Meanwhile, grate the carrots. Heat the ghee in a frying pan. Add the
grated carrots and gently fry for 5 minutes or until lightly golden.
3 Tip the carrots into a blender, add the sugar and 4–5 tbsp of the hot milk
and process to a coarse paste. Add this to the simmering milk and stir well.
Continue cooking over a low heat for a further 10 minutes.
4 Meanwhile, roughly grind the pistachios using a small spice mill or pestle
and mortar. Add to the simmering carrot mixture with the chopped almonds,
then mix in the saffron milk and cardamom. Simmer for a few more
minutes, then take off the heat. Serve hot or cold, topped with shredded
almonds and pistachio nuts if you like.

Strawberry and banana pudding

Illustrated on previous page

Serves 4
5 tbsp ghee
50g (2oz) cashew nuts
50g (2oz) raisins
150g (5oz) palm sugar

400ml (14fl oz) coconut milk
pinch of ground cardamom
250g (9oz) strawberries, sliced
2 bananas, peeled and chopped

1 Heat 3 tbsp ghee in a frying pan. Add the cashew nuts and fry for 2–3 minutes or until golden, adding the raisins after 1–2 minutes so that they plump up slightly. Remove the pan from the heat and set aside.
2 Put the palm sugar in a saucepan with 250ml (8fl oz) water and place over a low heat. Stir until the sugar dissolves, then increase the heat and simmer for 5 minutes. Add 2 tbsp ghee and continue cooking for a further 5 minutes or until the sauce thickens.
3 Lower the heat, add the coconut milk and simmer gently, stirring occasionally, for 10 minutes. Stir in the cardamom, then add the toasted cashew nuts and raisins. Remove the pan from the heat. Gently stir the strawberries and bananas into the sauce and set aside to cool before serving.

You can use any ripe fruit for this easy dessert, but I love the combination of banana and strawberries.

Vermicelli pudding

Serves 4

200g (7oz) vermicelli
6 tbsp ghee
50g (2oz) cashew nuts
50g (2oz) raisins
1.2 litres (2 pints) milk
150g (5oz) caster sugar
pinch of powdered saffron

1 Break up the vermicelli into short pieces, about 3cm (1¼ inches) long, and set aside.
2 Heat the ghee in a large frying pan. Add the cashew nuts and gently fry for 2–3 minutes or until golden. Remove from the frying pan using a slotted spoon and set aside to drain on kitchen paper.
3 Add the raisins to the frying pan and fry, stirring, for 1 minute or until they are plump and toasted. Transfer them to the kitchen paper with a slotted spoon. Add the vermicelli to the frying pan and cook for 5 minutes or until it turns brown.
4 Bring the milk to the boil in a large, heavy-based saucepan over a medium heat. Simmer, stirring constantly, for 20 minutes or until the milk has reduced in volume by half. Lower the heat, then add the vermicelli and cook, stirring constantly, for 15 minutes.
5 Add the sugar, cashew nuts, raisins and saffron. Simmer, stirring, for 5 minutes or until thoroughly blended. Serve the vermicelli pudding hot.

This dessert is very popular in South India, especially among Tamil people. It is often presented as part of a thali meal in restaurants specialising in Tamil cuisine, which can be found all over India.

Panchamritham

Serves 4
1 banana
1 plantain
1 mango
3 tbsp ghee
50g (2oz) raisins

50g (2oz) fresh dates, halved and
   stoned
50g (2oz) granulated sugar
3 tbsp thin honey
pinch of ground cardamom

1 Peel and roughly chop the banana and plantain. Halve the mango, cut the flesh away from the stone, then cut into cubes and set aside.
2 Heat the ghee in a large frying pan. Add the banana, plantain, raisins, dates and sugar and fry gently for 5 minutes or until the mixture browns slightly and the fruits are well blended with the ghee.
3 Remove the pan from the heat, add the honey, mango and ground cardamom and mix well. Set aside to cool, then chill until ready to serve.

Panchamritham is a traditional dessert from Tamil Nadu in South India. It is simple to make and has a good clean taste of honey and fruits. If plantain is unobtainable, simply use two bananas rather than one.

Mango halwa

Illustrated on previous pages

Serves 4–6
4 tbsp ghee
50g (2oz) freshly grated coconut
50g (2oz) semolina
450g (1lb) well drained, canned
    mango
150g (5oz) caster sugar, plus extra
    to sprinkle
200g (7oz) fresh mango flesh (about
    1 large mango), diced and well
    drained
1 tsp ground cardamom
chopped pistachio nuts, to serve

1 Heat 1 tbsp ghee in a large frying pan. Add the coconut and fry for
3 minutes or until golden. Remove with a slotted spoon and set aside to
drain on kitchen paper. Add the semolina to the frying pan and cook over a
low heat for 5 minutes or until golden. Remove from the pan and set aside.
Purée the canned mango pieces in a blender or food processor to give 450g
(1lb) pulp.
2 Put the sugar and 600ml (1 pint) water in a large, heavy-based saucepan.
Heat slowly, stirring until the sugar dissolves, then increase the heat and
bring to the boil. Add the mango pulp and 2 tbsp ghee. Turn the heat down
to medium and cook for 35 minutes until well reduced, stirring frequently to
prevent the mixture sticking to the pan.
3 Add the remaining 1 tbsp of ghee and cook for a further 15 minutes,
stirring frequently, until the mixture is very thick. Sprinkle in the toasted
semolina and cook for a further 15 minutes or until the mixture is smooth
and comes away easily from the sides of the pan.
4 Add the fresh mango, toasted coconut and cardamom. Stir well, then pour
the mixture into an oiled baking tin, about 25 x 20 cm (10 x 8 inches). Leave
to cool, then chill overnight until set. Cut into pieces and serve cold or at
room temperature, sprinkled with pistachios and a little extra sugar.

Halwa originates from North India and is generally time-consuming to make, but I have created a simplified version. It has a delicious flavour and soft texture.

Saffron kulfi

Illustrated on page 282

8–10 servings
4 litres (7 pints) milk
1 tbsp rice flour
175g (6oz) caster sugar
1 tsp saffron threads

1 Bring the milk to the boil in a heavy-based saucepan. Lower the heat
slightly and simmer for 45 minutes or until thickened and reduced by half.
Remove from the heat and leave to cool slightly.
2 In a bowl, mix the rice flour with 2 tbsp of the milk until smooth. Pour in
the warm milk, stirring constantly, then return to the pan. Cook, stirring,
for 15 minutes or until the milk has reduced to the consistency of a pouring
sauce. Add the sugar and saffron threads and stir until the sugar has
dissolved. Leave to cool completely.
3 Transfer to a freezerproof container and place in the freezer for 1 hour,
then remove and whisk well to break down the ice crystals. Return to the
freezer for another hour, then repeat the whisking and freezing process
twice more. Finally freeze the kulfi, in individual moulds if you like, for
4–5 hours or overnight.
4 Soften the kulfi at room temperature for 5 minutes before serving.

Kulfi, India's famously rich ice cream, is a
regular feature on every Indian restaurant
menu in Britain, but back home it is a cooling
streetfood, sold by kulfi-sellers on bicycles.

Almond kulfi

8–10 servings
4 litres (7 pints) milk
1 tbsp rice flour
175g (6oz) caster sugar
25g (1oz) ground almonds

25g (1oz) sliced almonds
few drops of almond extract
150ml (¼ pint) double cream, lightly
   whipped

1 Bring the milk to the boil in a heavy-based saucepan. Lower the heat slightly and simmer for 45 minutes or until thickened and reduced by half. Remove from the heat and leave to cool slightly.

2 In a bowl, mix the rice flour with 2 tbsp of the milk until smooth. Pour in the warm milk, stirring constantly, then return to the pan. Cock, stirring, for 15 minutes or until the milk has reduced to the consistency of a pouring sauce. Add the sugar and stir until dissolved. Leave to cool completely.

3 Fold the ground almonds, sliced almonds and almond extract into the cooled kulfi base, followed by the lightly whipped cream.

4 Transfer to a freezerproof container and place in the freezer for 1 hour, then remove and whisk well to break down the ice crystals. Return to the freezer for another hour, then repeat the whisking and freezing process twice more. Finally freeze the kulfi, in individual moulds if you like, for 4–5 hours or overnight.

5 Soften the kulfi at room temperature for 5 minutes before serving.

Kulfi was first prepared for the grand Moguls in clay pots, but today metal moulds are more common. Either freeze the kulfi in individual 175ml (6fl oz) moulds, or in a large container – slicing the ice cream to serve.

Mango kulfi

8–10 servings
4 litres (7 pints) milk
1 tbsp rice flour
175g (6oz) caster sugar
410g can mango pieces, drained
pinch of ground cardamom
150ml (¼ pint) double cream, lightly
   whipped
1 small mango, diced, to serve
   (optional)

1 Bring the milk to the boil in a heavy-based saucepan. Lower the heat slightly and simmer for 45 minutes or until thickened and reduced by half. Remove from the heat and leave to cool slightly.
2 In a bowl, mix the rice flour with 2 tbsp of the milk until smooth. Pour in the warm milk, stirring constantly, then return to the pan. Cook, stirring, for 15 minutes or until the milk has reduced to the consistency of a pouring sauce. Add the sugar and stir until dissolved. Leave to cool completely.
3 Purée the mango in a blender until smooth. Measure 150ml (¼ pint) mango purée and stir in the cardamom. Fold this into the kulfi base, then fold in the lightly whipped cream.
4 Transfer to a freezerproof container and place in the freezer for 1 hour, then remove and whisk well to break down the ice crystals. Return to the freezer for another hour, then repeat the whisking and freezing process twice more. Finally freeze the kulfi in one large container or individual moulds if you prefer, for 4–5 hours or overnight.
5 Soften the kulfi at room temperature for 5 minutes before slicing to serve. Scatter with diced fresh mango if you like.

Pistachio kulfi

8–10 servings
4 litres (7 pints) milk
1 tbsp rice flour
175g (6oz) caster sugar
50g (2oz) pistachio nuts, skinned
   and crushed, plus extra to serve
few drops of rose water
150ml (¼ pint) double cream, lightly
   whipped

1 Bring the milk to the boil in a heavy-based saucepan. Lower the heat slightly and simmer for 45 minutes or until thickened and reduced by half. Remove from the heat and leave to cool slightly.
2 In a bowl, mix the rice flour with 2 tbsp of the milk until smooth. Pour in the warm milk, stirring constantly, then return to the pan. Cook, stirring, for 15 minutes or until the milk has reduced to the consistency of a pouring sauce. Add the sugar and stir until dissolved. Leave to cool completely.
3 Add the crushed pistachio nuts and rose water to the cooled kulfi base, mix well, then fold in the lightly whipped cream.
4 Transfer to a freezerproof container and place in the freezer for 1 hour, then remove and whisk well to break down the ice crystals. Return to the freezer for another hour, then repeat the whisking and freezing process twice more. Finally freeze the kulfi in individual 175ml (6fl oz) moulds for 4–5 hours or overnight.
5 Soften the kulfi at room temperature for 5 minutes before turning out on to individual plates. Scatter with crushed pistachios to serve.

Fruit flavoured kulfi tend to vary according to what is in season, but kulfi based on nuts and spices are made all year round.

Keralan lassi

Serves 3–4
300g (11oz) natural yogurt
2.5cm (1 inch) piece fresh root
   ginger, peeled and sliced
2–3 shallots, peeled and sliced
2 green chillies, chopped
few curry leaves
pinch of cumin seeds
pinch of ground cumin
sea salt

1 Place the yogurt, ginger, shallots, chopped chillies, curry leaves and a little salt in a blender. Add 300ml (½ pint) water and process until smooth and thoroughly blended. Pour into a jug and chill until ready to serve.
2 Briefly toast the cumin seeds in a dry frying pan over a medium heat until fragrant, then remove from the heat.
3 When ready to serve, place some crushed ice in each glass, pour in the lassi and sprinkle with the ground cumin and toasted cumin seeds.

In Kerala, this is the drink you will be offered on a hot afternoon. The fresh taste of spices with clean, thin yogurt is truly refreshing.

Banana lassi

Serves 2–4
250g (9oz) natural yogurt
200g (7oz) banana, cubed
125ml (4fl oz) milk
4 tsp sugar
½ tsp ground cardamom
1 tbsp pistachio nuts, crushed

1 Place the yogurt, banana, milk and sugar in a blender and blend until very smooth. Stir in the ground cardamom.
2 Place some crushed ice in a serving jug or individual glasses and pour the lassi over. Sprinkle with the crushed pistachio nuts and serve.

This is one of my favourite drinks – the thought of flavourful bananas blended with cold yogurt, sugar and a touch of cardamom always makes my mouth water.

Almond milk shake

Serves 4
2 tbsp blanched almonds
2 tbsp pistachio nuts
450ml (¾ pint) milk
2 tbsp brown sugar
½ tsp ground cardamom

1 Place the almonds and pistachio nuts in a blender, add 100ml (3½fl cz) water and work to a coarse paste. Add the milk and brown sugar and process for a further 2 minutes or until smooth and well blended.
2 Divide the milk shake among 4 serving glasses. Add some crushed ice, then sprinkle with ground cardamom and serve immediately.

I am very partial to this Indian-style milk shake. It's a lovely combination of flavours and is very refreshing served chilled.

Tangy carrot juice

Serves 4
500g (1lb 2oz) carrots, peeled
2.5cm (1 inch) piece fresh root
    ginger, peeled and chopped
1 tbsp mint leaves
2 tbsp lime juice
sea salt

1 Cut the carrots into chunks, then push them through a juice extractor
with the chopped ginger and mint leaves. Transfer the carrot juice to a jug,
add sea salt to taste and the lime juice. Chill before serving.

New Delhi juice bars offer the best selection of
drinks I have ever seen. I am fascinated by the
clever North Indian use of spices to make
interesting drinks. My favourite flavourings
for carrot juice are fresh mint and ginger.

Cardamom tea

Serves 4

275ml (9fl oz) milk

2 tbsp Assam tea leaves

2.5cm (1 inch) piece fresh root
   ginger, peeled and grated

5 green cardamom pods

sugar, to taste

1 Pour the milk into a small saucepan, add 275ml (9fl oz) water and bring to the boil. Lower the heat slightly and add the tea leaves, ginger, cardamom and sugar to taste. Simmer gently for 5 minutes, stirring occasionally to ensure that the ingredients are well mixed.

2 Remove the pan from the heat and discard the cardamom pods. Pour the cardamom tea into cups and serve immediately.

Spiced milky tea is hugely popular in India and can be made with either complex spice blends or simple ones. This version is made using green cardamom pods, which have a sweet lemony flavour, plus fresh ginger. For authenticity, use Assam tea.

Watermelon and lime juice

Serves 4
½ watermelon
2 tbsp lime juice
1–2 tbsp sugar, to taste (optional)
4 thin lime slices

1 Cut away the rind from the watermelon and remove the seeds with a teaspoon. Cut the flesh into manageable pieces. Push the watermelon flesh through a juice extractor. Alternatively, you can purée the watermelon in a blender, then sieve the juice.
2 Transfer the watermelon juice to a jug and add the lime juice. Taste and sweeten with a little sugar, if required, mixing well. Chill the juice in the refrigerator until ready to serve.
3 To serve, pour the chilled watermelon juice into 4 serving glasses. Add some crushed ice and a lime slice to each glass.

On a scorching hot summer's day, there is nothing more refreshing than this wonderful fruit juice.

Index